TOWARDS A CHRISTIAN
UNDERSTANDING

The Pursuit of a Christian Philosophy

STEVEN R. MARTINS

FOREWORD BY
Adolfo García de la Sienra Guajardo

To my third son, Nehemías Agustín,
may the LORD *God lead you in all truth*

This book is a wonderful invitation to a rediscovery not only of philosophy as a discipline but of a way of seeing the world. Distinctly Christian in his approach, and personal in his content, Martins shows us the scope of God's creative and redemptive powers when it comes to our understanding of the created order. Martins introduces the dutch philosopher Herman Dooyeweerd in a way that invites us to an integrated perspective, describing the implications of his ideas to all aspects of life, such as the sciences, culture and our practical living. I highly recommend this book.

Josué Reichow
L'Abri Fellowship (UK)
Author of *Reform Your Mind*

Towards a Christian Understanding: The Pursuit of a Christian Philosophy by Steven R. Martins is an eye-opening introduction to a misunderstood and greatly ignored subject in 21st Century Christendom. The biblical gospel message is a holistic, not only eschatological and soteriological, kingdom-message for the exaltation of the glory of the King Jesus that must permeate every realm of our being, thoughts, and motives, as well as how we evaluate the world around us.

This book will help the reader understand what a true Christian philosophy is, what a biblical worldview (or "world-and-life view") is, and how they both relate to each other. Furthermore, Steven carefully breaks down the false dichotomy wrongly forged between theology and life that we have inherited from our Post-Enlightenment Western world. Upon completion, the careful reader should be able to re-evaluate not only what it means to be a Christian in God's kingdom and to think from God's kingdom mandates, but also how to evaluate the flawed reasoning of the unregenerate world systems around us, and finally lament and reject their influence in contemporary Christian thought.

Joseph Owen
Answers in Genesis (LATAM)
Petersburg, Kentucky, USA

All the treasures of wisdom and knowledge are found in Christ (Col. 2:3). Therefore, Paul warned the Christians at Colossae about a type of philosophy based on human wisdom rather than Christ which could take them captive (Col. 2:8). When Christians try to build their philosophical system on supposedly "neutral" ground or anything other than Christ it is a foundation set on sinking sand. Steven R. Martins has here written a short booklet which helps the Christian understand what is a truly Christian and Biblical understanding of philosophy drawing from some of the finest Reformed and Presuppositional thinkers. In a day with many ideological threats such as postmodernism, cultural Marxism, naturalism, and compromised 'Christian' worldviews, there is a real need for intentional thinking and discipleship in this area. Though this is a little book, it is no lightweight reading. It contributes to equipping the reader with an understanding of categories of thought and foundations to build upon with a wealth of sources to continue one's growth. Martins has managed to pack a lot into this little package for the deep-thinking Christian to ponder.

Thaddeus Maharaj, B.F.A., M.TS
Founder and author at THEOTIVITY.COM,
Director of Media & Discipleship,
Hope Church Toronto West

TOWARDS A CHRISTIAN
UNDERSTANDING

The Pursuit of a Christian Philosophy

STEVEN R. MARTINS

FOREWORD BY
Adolfo García de la Sienra Guajardo

cp

cántaro
publications

cántaro
publications

www.cantaroinstitute.org

Towards a Christian Understanding:
The Pursuit of a Christian Philosophy
by Steven R. Martins

Published by Cántaro Publications, a publishing imprint of
the Cántaro Institute, Jordan Station, ON.

Book design by Cántaro Institute

Library & Archives Canada

ISBN 978-1-990771-03-3

Printed in the United States of America

CONTENTS

EXPANDED
CONTENTS

FOREWORD

WRITTEN IN BRISK ENGLISH but with the typical pregnant style of Spanish sentences, this book presents in a very compact, albeit complete way, the essentials of the philosophy of the law idea, also known as Reformational Philosophy (RP). There is no doubt that it accomplishes its objective, namely "to introduce you to a philosophy that has the God of Christian theism as the ultimate starting point of all thinking, a philosophy that is *distinctly* Christian, free from the pagan influence of this fallen world's philosophies." This book must be seen as a primer of Christian philosophy, helping those who discover the rich treasure of RP to become acquainted with its principles and method.

As it is common among well-educated Hispanic-Americans, Martins' original background was Scholastic, since Hispanic-America was built upon the foundations of Scholastic thought, both Thomist and Suarecian.[1] But the influence of the Jesuit Francisco Suárez (in particular) is not alien to the history of Dutch Calvinism. Up to roughly the time of the Peace of Westphalia, the Dutch Calvinists were also trained in Suárez's philosophy, as the standard prolegomena

---

1.   Cf. García de la Sienra, A., and L. Rodríguez Medina (2012), "Hispanic-American Philosophy in the Fringes of the Empire" in K. Brzechczyn and K. Paprzycka (eds.), *Thinking About Provincialism in Thinking* (Poznan Studies in the Philosophy of the Sciences and the Humanities, 100). Amsterdam/New York: Rodopi.

for Reformed theology in the Netherlands were the *Metaphysical Disputations* of the Spanish philosopher.[2] Actually, the famous Dutch poet Jacob Revius published in 1644 a compendium*, Suarez repurgatus,* in order to present prolegomena that he considered more apt for Reformed theology.[3] Hence, it is only natural for someone formed in the great Spanish Scholastic tradition to make the transition into a more Biblical worldview and specifically into RP. This is happening at large in Hispanic-America nowadays, where students of Reformed theology have found the treasure of RP and are making a smooth transition from their previous background into it.

The search for philosophical prolegomena to theology that constitutes, at the same time, a full-fledged philosophical theory is common to the Roman Catholic and the Calvinist traditions; only these have developed monumental philosophical theories that intend to have Christian bases. In this book Martins presents a response to this most important question: Why is a Christian philosophy vital for our Christian living? He discusses then what is philosophy, what is a properly Christian philosophy, and why it is important for Christians.

From a presuppositionalist point of view, influenced by Cornelius van Til, Martins explains what faith is, and how it induces a worldview which in turn is the starting point of philosophy. He claims that no one can have a philoso-

---

2. Suárez, F. (1597), *Disputationes metaphysicae.* Salamanca: Imprenta de Juan y Andrés Renaut.

3. Revius, J. (1644), *Suarez repurgatus. Sive syllabus disputationum metaphysicarum Francisci Suarez. Cum notis.* Leiden: Franciscum Hegerum.

phy without a previous worldview. His distinction between faith and religion is important. Faith is a deep belief about the nature of the Ultimate Ground of reality, of the divine (and, I would add: and of the proper relation to it), and so it is necessarily religious. The way Martins sees the relation between faith and philosophy is as follows:

> In summary, all scientific (theoretical) knowledge is rooted in a person's philosophy (or philosophical convictions), the mother of all sciences, which is in turn rooted in a person's worldview, and that worldview is rooted in a person's faith (*supra*-rational conviction), which by definition is religious in nature.

In the second chapter Martins introduces Herman Dooyeweerd, who is the first philosopher in the history of the discipline that introduced a novel, non-Scholastic approach to Christian philosophy. In the remaining three chapters, Martins introduces the main tenets of Dooyeweerd's philosophy in a concise but complete way. The book is an excellent introduction to this growing school of thought, as it explains the concepts of RP in a very clear way. Particularly outstanding is his discussion on general and special revelation, as well as his discussion on the mathematical modalities, but the reader will surely find in this book a very cogent and systematic exposition of RP.

Adolfo García de la Sienra
Universidad Veracruzana
Xalapa, Veracruz
Mexico

INTRODUCTION

THE SMALL BOOK YOU HOLD in your hands is a humble effort of a Christian thinker and devout student to introduce to you an *understanding* that has remained for the most part widely neglected or treated as altogether foreign by many in the church past and present. What I mean by "understanding" is an understanding of creation, of all reality, that which is seen and unseen – most particularly a *Christian* understanding. You might be with me up to this point, but I urge you to continue after I make the following clarification: By an "understanding of creation" (or of cosmic reality), I do not mean a *theological* understanding, I mean a Christian *philosophical* understanding, or put more simply, a *Christian philosophy*.

Christian? Philosophy? Seldom have we heard those two words together, and when we have, it has often been in reference to the medieval scholastics of the Roman Catholic church, or to some of the church's historic apologists who have done nothing more than regurgitate the philosophical argumentation of the ancients. No, scholasticism is not what I mean, nor do I mean the philosophy espoused and employed by William Lane Craig (b. 1949–), for example, who has garnered quite a following for himself as a supposedly *Christian* philosopher. As it concerns scholasticism, I have no intention of introducing to you a thought system that treats man's natural knowledge as on par with the divine revelation of God. And as it concerns William Lane Craig, I have no intention of introducing to you a philosophy that is not *informed* by, nor *presupposes,* the divine revelation of God (sorry to all you Christian rationalists!).[1] It is not that there is nothing of value to be found in the writings of Socrates, Plato, Aristotle, etc., or even in the teachings of Craig, it is that their philosophical systems as a *whole* are all wrong, they do not have the correct ultimate starting point epistemically that permits them to see reality for what it truly is, and to therefore interpret it in a manner that is consistent with the divine revelation of God. No, my objective is to introduce to you a philosophy that has the God of Christian theism as the ultimate starting point for all thinking, a philosophy that is *distinctly* Christian, free from the pagan influence of this fallen world's philosophies.

Being of Ibero-American descent, I was very much influenced by the scholastic manner of thinking in my upbringing. When I wanted to learn something about God, my personal salvation, sanctification, and any and everything having to do with the spiritual, I would pick up my Bible and turn to the writings and teachings of Christian

---

1. Christians can be "rational", but they cannot adopt "rational*ism*" and expect to be found consistent with their biblical worldview in their thinking, this epistemic view regards *reason* (and what is that anyways? The abstract concept of "reason" is *not* "understanding") as the chief source and test of knowledge, taking the place of God as the ultimate authority for all knowledge. See H. Evan Runner, *Walking in the Way of the Word: The Collected Writings of H. Evan Runner*, ed. Kerry J. Hollingsworth (Grand Rapids, MI.: The Reformational Publishing Project, 2009), 60.

theologians. But when I wanted to learn about the world in general, I would turn to the philosophers of ancient Greece and work my way up to the period of the Enlightenment. It was as if I lived in two separate realms, the realm of grace, and the realm of nature. And when I realized that these two realms were for the most part irreconcilable (I really could not align what I was reading in Scripture with what I was reading in academia), I attempted to solve this dilemma by committing a grave error in my thinking, elevating *theology* as the queen of the sciences. I desired a cogent and biblically faithful understanding of the world, and what I had done, particularly in attempting to have *theology* answer *philosophical* questions, was create more questions and thus confusion. The Bible was not given to us by God to serve as a textbook for any of the scientific enterprises of man, I learned that rather quickly, but the alternative that I was faced with did not seem the right course of action either, which was to disregard the Bible altogether. What was my dilemma? That what I had read and learned in God's Word was not corresponding and aligning with what I was experiencing and learning in the world. Something had to give. And what was it that had to give? You might be surprised to know the answer: My (truncated) understanding of the gospel.

For most of my spiritual upbringing, I had been taught that the gospel was nothing more than the salvation of our souls from hell and judgment by the grace of God. While I believed that Jesus was my *Lord* and *Saviour*, I did not yet fully understand the far-reaching implications of Jesus' title of "Lord" (Gk. *Kurios*), and its relation to the title of "Saviour". My understanding was, for the most part, incomplete, and when I discovered the biblical meaning of Christ's

Lordship, not as some future millennial reign, or even solely in a spiritual sense, but as the Sovereign Ruler over all creation, suddenly my eyes were opened. If Jesus is Lord over all creation, if He is reigning now presently, if the millennium is symbolic for the church age (see St. Augustine's twentieth chapter in his book *The City of God*), then salvation must be more than just our spiritual salvation, it must extend to the whole of the created cosmos. Suddenly, I was seeing the gospel's promise of *redemption* and *renewal* in a new light. And with a more fully fleshed out understanding of Christ's Lordship, I began to understand that there was nothing truly that was outside of Christ's dominion, that included *philosophy*.

The four most memorable events of my life have been (i) my salvation, (ii) my marriage to my wife Cindy, (iii) the birth of our boys Matthias, Timothy, and Nehemías, and (iv) my discovery of how my faith in Christ related to every sphere of life. In regard to the fourth, the Lord God, according to His divine providence, used the discipline of apologetics to help me discover the comprehensive nature of the gospel. Some of the individuals who helped me in this journey have been those who have gone to be with the Lord before this journey had even begun, such as Cornelius Van Til, Greg L. Bahnsen, and R.J. Rushdoony, as well as those who are still here with us, such as John M. Frame (through his writings) and Joseph Boot (through his personal tutelage). And this is still very much a journey for me even now, for having served for twelve years in ministry – at times as an itinerant apologist, other times as a writer, and presently as the director of the Cántaro Institute, project manager of Paideia Press, and founding pastor of Sevilla Chapel in

St. Catharines, Ontario, Canada – I still persist each day to grow in my understanding of the world, my place in it, and of the God who holds all things in His hands. Each day I can repeat with added force the words of Abraham Kuyper:

> No single piece of our mental world is to be hermetically sealed off from the rest, and there is not a square inch in the whole domain of our human existence over which Christ, who is Sovereign over all, does not cry: Mine![2]

I have written this book for you, therefore, to help you discover what I am *still* discovering, and what will likely be a whole lifetime of discovery. I do not write to you as one who has mastered Christian philosophy – not by any means! – but I am no longer as one left in the dark. I am a student, and will remain a student until the day I die, and so consider me a devout student inviting you, another student, or an explorer inviting another explorer, to join me in this journey of discovering Christian philosophy. You will notice, as you read on further, that I am unashamedly a presuppositionalist as it relates to my apologetic, this is because I do not believe you can be an evidentialist or a rationalist and yet hold to a *Christian* philosophy, the only way forward is as a presuppositionalist. If you disagree, well, do not let that stop you from reading this book, and I urge you to consider what I have to say on the matter when I touch on it in the second chapter.

What can you expect from this book then? In the first

---

2. Abraham Kuyper, inaugural lecture at the Free University of Amsterdam, October 20, 1880, quoted in *Abraham Kuyper: A Centennial Reader*, ed. James D. Bratt (Grand Rapids: Eerdmans, 1998), 488.

chapter, I set out to answer the question What is philosophy? And whether there can truly be such a thing as a *Christian* philosophy. In the second chapter, I introduce the person who first developed and introduced a distinctly *Christian* philosophy in the Netherlands, Herman Dooyeweerd, and how the philosophers of the past can be understood in light of Dooyeweerd's philosophy. In the third chapter, I seek to answer What is thus a distinctly *Christian* view (or under-standing) of creational (cosmic) reality? And in the fourth chapter, how we ought to understand the law-order of cre-ational (cosmic) reality. And finally, in the fifth chapter, the answer to perhaps the most important question, Why is a Christian philosophy vital for our Christian living? I may as well go as far as to say that this chapter is the *whole point* of this book. Without it, you will not understand how all this ties together.

As you read on, you will notice that this small book was not written as a textbook for Christian philosophy, it was never meant to be, hence why there are many other com-plex components of Dooyeweerdian philosophy that are not covered in this publication. Instead, this book is meant to be a *primer* for Christian philosophy, so that, for some of you, this may be where you begin your own journey towards developing a Christian understanding of creational (cosmic) reality. Thus, if by the end of this book I have succeeded in piquing your interest, and motivating you to study further under the greats of Christian philosophy past and present, then this publication has served its purpose.

Soli Deo Gloria

Steven R. Martins
Niagara, ON., 2021

THE PURSUIT
OF A CHRISTIAN
PHILOSOPHY

1.1 What is Philosophy?

WHEN WE MENTION the term "philosophy", the first thought that might come to mind are the ancient Greek philosophers, such as Socrates, Plato, Aristotle, or the lesser philosophers. If you are not as well acquainted with ancient Greek philosophy, and find yourself more acquainted with the corporate world, for example, you might instead think about business philosophy, political philosophy, or the "general way of doing things." When a corporate spokesperson, or government official, refers to their "philosophy", they most often than not are referring to how they do things, and perhaps even the why. The term certainly could be used within these contexts, but if you were to ask what philosophy actually *is*, these references do not prove to be quite helpful. The ancient Greek philosophers certainly come closer to helping us understand what philosophy *is* in comparison to how our modern culture has treated the term. They were the ones, after all, who were historically celebrated for their philosophical inquiries. You say the word "philosophy", and you associate the term with ancient Greece. But even then, even if we were to read the Greek philosophers, we would not have a clear definition of what philosophy *is*. What then *is* philosophy?

Philosophy is a theoretical enterprise, it is a science, and as one scholar would put it, it is "the discipline of the disciplines",[1] or as another would say, "the mother of all sciences."[2] While we could certainly examine philosophy in other ways, including the practical, as mentioned above in the corporate and/or political example, our interest is primarily in philosophy as a *science*. And when I use the term "science", I do mean it in the broad sense of the term, which extends *beyond* the natural sciences and includes such things as the humanities (including theology). When we ask questions such as, What is philosophy? What makes philosophy a science? What is science? And how does philosophy, as a theoretical enterprise, as a science, differ from what one might call practical knowledge? We are essentially engaging in philosophy, we are *philosophizing*. You might think that such philosophizing is irrelevant, or unnecessary for your daily living, and with the worsening degeneration of the West's intellectual climate, the majority in our society might actually agree with you. But philosophy is incredibly relevant, necessary even, for our daily living. In fact, it is inescapable. On that matter I will return. But there is a follow up question to that of "What *is* philosophy?"

---

1. See D.F.M. Strauss, *Philosophy: The Discipline of the Disciplines* (Jordan Station, ON.: Paideia Press, 2021), 59.

2. See Willem J. Ouweneel, *Wisdom for Thinkers: An Introduction to Christian Philosophy* (Jordan Station, ON.: Paideia Press, 2014), 1.

1.2 Is there such a thing as a Christian Philosophy?

Is there such a thing as a *Christian* philosophy? The idea runs contrary to what we are accustomed to in our "secular" world. It would be like asking whether a fry cook could be a *Christian* fry cook, in the sense that there might be some *Christian way* of being a fry cook. Or whether a medical practitioner could be a *Christian* medical practitioner. The artificial sacred-secular divide that our culture has developed and embraced has left us scratching our heads just trying to imagine whether such things could possibly exist. The matter of "religion" or "religious beliefs" are supposedly reserved for the *private* sphere of one's life, and thus positing the idea of a *Christian* philosophy, of a *Christian* theoretical enterprise, would be like mixing oil with water when philosophy is supposedly placed in the *public* sphere. But this understanding is a false one because it is, in fact, artificial. In other words, it is a divide, a dualism, that was concocted by the minds of men and imposed upon Western society, and being artificial as opposed to real, it does not prove itself to be a true understanding of the world and how we operate in it.[3] As we shall see, the notion of religious neutrality, of objective, unbiased understanding inherent to the present sacred-secular divide, is an impossibility both in theory and in practicality.

1.3 Why does Philosophy, or Christian Philosophy, matter?

As I had mentioned, we are all involved in one form or another in *philosophizing*. Architects, for example, have to

---

3. See Mark L. Ward, Biblical Worldview: Creation, Fall, Redemption (Greenville, SC.: BJU Press, 2016), 34-36.

study architecture in order to be able to fulfill their tasks
as architects. How else, for example, could a three-storey
house, or a school building, be built if not without an architectural design? And there is certainly a difference between an architect and a general labourer who attempts to
draw and build something of his own making. A building
company will not hire just about anyone to be an architect,
but someone who is well attuned to the sciences involved in
architecture. An architect, for example, would have studied
mathematics, including geometry, algebra, trigonometry,
and calculus, as well physics, engineering, computer science,
and art. Has anyone, whether the architect, or the company
hiring one, ever asked themselves what makes these sciences
"scientific"? Why are they each called "sciences"? And how
does the architect differ from the practical insights of the
general labourer? If you think that these questions are "architectural" questions, you might be surprised to learn that
they are not. These are, in fact, *philosophical* questions. Because of the fact that architectural design is intricately inter-
twined with mathematics, physics, and engineering, on the
one hand, and cultural sciences on the other, architectural
design is therefore founded on both (i) natural and (ii) cultural philosophy.[4]

Irregardless as to what kind of science one decides to
engage in, whether natural, cultural, or human, if he or she
wants to do it well, he or she cannot possibly do so without asking the most fundamental questions, such as: What
is science? What is nature? What is culture? What is man?
Essentially, the "What is…" questions. And these questions
are unavoidable for the one who seeks to engage in these

4.   Ouweneel, *Wisdom for Thinkers*, 3.

natural, cultural, or human sciences *thoroughly*. How could the architect, for example, possibly draw building plans if he does not even know what a building is, or what building plans are, or what design itself is? Admittedly, the architect does go about drawing his building plans whether or not he has philosophized these matters, and that is because he already has some vague idea about these things in the back of his mind. He is not, after all, absolutely clueless, otherwise he would never have become an architect.

While architecture can certainly explain aspects relating to itself, it cannot explain its own nature. Architecture is both the art and science of designing buildings and structures, but in order to explain its nature, what we need is another science, and that science is the science of sciences, the discipline of disciplines: philosophy. If we want to understand architecture, we have to first ask the question: What is science? And then, what are architectural phenomena?[5] Whether with one or the other, you are engaging in philosophy, and thus, philosophy proves to be unavoidable, inescapable, inevitable.

1.4 Worldviews, Beliefs, and Faith

We still have a way to go toward understanding what philosophy is, however. If philosophy is a science, the mother of all the sciences, we need to know what "science" is. Science

---

5. Defined as "the manipulation of space, material, and light and shadow to create a memorable encounter through an impact on the human senses…" in "Theory of Phenomenology: Analyzing Substance, Application, and Influence.pdf", *The University of Kansas* [not dated]. Accessed September 28, 2021, https://cte.ku.edu/sites/cte.drupal.ku.edu/files/docs/portfolios/kraus/essay2.pdf

is a theoretical (and thus specific) form of knowledge, which means that it forms part of the wider field of what we call "epistemology", or the philosophy of knowledge. This is the first of three aspects of philosophy, and this first aspect concerns how we know what we know, and – of course – what is knowledge itself. The two other aspects are metaphysics and ethics, though for some philosophers, the term "metaphysics" is exchanged with "ontology", which is the philosophy of *being*, or of all things that exist, the totality of the created cosmos, in other words. While ethics can be understood as the philosophy of moral principles, essentially what is morally good and bad, and what is morally right and wrong. If you are familiar with Cornelius Van Til (1895-1987), and his successors Greg L. Bahnsen (1948-1995) and John M. Frame (b. 1939–), you may recall that these three aspects, epistemology, metaphysics, and ethics, are listed in their respective publications as components of the Christian philosophy of life, or the Christian worldview.[6] Some philosophers have argued for epistemology and metaphysics/ontology while excluding ethics for the understanding of what philosophy is, but I hold to all three, adopting the "Triperspectivalism" put forward by Frame and Vern S. Poythress. While it was certainly Immanuel Kant (1724-1804) who initially argued for the inclusion of ethics, I prefer Frame and Poythress' biblical triperspectivalism, which emphasizes:

6.   See Cornelius Van Til, *Christian Apologetics* (Phillipsburg, NJ.: P&R Publishing Company, 2003); Greg L. Bahnsen, *Pushing the Antithesis*, ed. Gary DeMar (Powder Springs, GA.: American Vision, 2007); John M. Frame, *Apologetics: A Justification of Christian Belief* (Phillipsburg, NJ.: P&R Publishing, 2015).

the importance of a set of threefold distinctions, or triads…
Many people have seen a certain mystery in the number
three. But in Scripture there is a pervasive pattern of threefold distinctions which, though mysterious, provide us with
considerable illumination… a kind of deep structure of the
universe…[7]

But before we can begin to discuss worldview, we need
to answer the question of What is philosophy?, and with
the three aspects of philosophy already mentioned above, we
can answer that question by defining philosophy this way:
*Philosophy is the science (discipline) of the sciences (disciplines),
the foundational science (or discipline), that seeks to answer the
most basic of questions concerning our:*

1) *knowing (epistemology),*
2) *being (metaphysics/ontology),* and
3) *ethics (morality).*

The reason that philosophy is considered the mother of
all sciences is because it focuses on the *totality* of the created
order, or of reality, while the other sciences focus on various
parts of the created order, or of reality, separately.[8]

If, therefore, we understand philosophy to be the foundational science (discipline) for all the sciences (disciplines),
we are left with the question, What is that science (or discipline) founded on? It certainly cannot be on any other
science, because then philosophy would cease to be that
foundational science (or discipline). If not any other sci-

---

7. John M. Frame, What is Tri-Perspectivalism?, *Frame-Poyth-
ress*. Accessed September 28, 2021, https://frame-poythress.
org/what-is-triperspectivalism/.
8. Ouweneel, *Wisdom for Thinkers*, 6.

ence, what then? The answer might surprise you; it is neither philosophic or scientific in nature. The answer is *worldview*, or world-and-life view.

A worldview can be defined as a system of beliefs (or a network of presuppositions) concerning epistemology, metaphysics, and ethics – as laid out by Van Til, Bahnsen, and Frame – by which we interpret our human experience in God's created reality. Everyone has a worldview, although not everyone may have an understanding of philosophy, but while a person certainly could have a worldview without philosophy (think of a child, for example), he or she cannot have philosophy without a preceding worldview.

At this point, there needs to be some clarification as to the terms "worldview" and "faith", because many times the terms tend to be conflated into one, or one term is used in order to cancel out the other. Whereas one's philosophy is founded upon one's worldview, one's worldview is founded upon one's faith. It is true that when one makes reference to the Christian faith, he or she means the Christian worldview,[9] but while the two references may be used interchangeably in this sense, that is not what I mean by "faith" here. When there is a conflation of the two terms, "faith" and "worldview", what we really mean is the Christian religion, and on the term and matter of "religion" I will return. But faith here, as the foundation of one's worldview, is not meant in terms of a religion (or worldview). While our worldview can be described as rational, our faith can be described as *supra*-rational, in other words, it transcends

9. See F.L. Cross, ed., *The Oxford Dictionary of the Christian Church*, second edition (Toronto, ON.: Oxford University Press, 1974), 499.

reason (this does not mean that it is *irrational*). Think about it: The faith that underlies a person's worldview is certainly connected to one's affections, emotions, social relationships, linguistics, etc. But that faith is more than that, it transcends all that, it is above all that, hence why it is *supra*-rational.

Think of the human person. We are capable of physical, psychical, physiological, logical, social, economic, and moral functions, to name just a few. We can move, think, eat, reason, converse, negotiate, desire, and act, and so much more. Is that *all* that we are though? Are we the sum of all these parts? Or are we more? We believe we are more than just our functions. Who we are, our ego, our root-unity, is ultimately more than the sum of all these functions. If, therefore, my faith is *supra*-rational to my beliefs, that is to say, if it is *beyond* my beliefs, and if the human ego is *beyond* all of man's functions, then, as per the Dutch philosopher Willem J. Ouweneel: "faith is a matter of [the] ego, of [the] deepest self, beyond which there is nothing."[10] How then do we define "faith" in this instance? It is the deepest inner conviction of the human ego.

This is exactly why the unbeliever has a worldview that is antithetical to that of biblical Christianity: Because in spite of believing what ultimately does not correspond to reality, essentially what cannot be made sense of from his or her set of presuppositions – because they do not provide the pre-conditions for intelligibility[11] – the unbeliever has a deep inner conviction that has been corrupted by the power of sin, and, therefore, is always antagonistic towards the

---

10. Ouweneel, *Wisdom for Thinkers*, 10.
11. The process of predication, that is, making sense of the intelligibility of reality.

truth (of God).

1.5 Distinguishing between Faith and Religion

The apostle Paul writes that unbelievers "by their unrighteousness suppress the truth" (Rom. 1:18b), and by this we understand that man's faith is always religious, or to put it another way, that faith always "possesses a religious nature."[12] While the term "religion" can be used in various contexts to mean various things, in one context, for example, it may refer to a worldview; in another context, it may refer to works-based righteousness; in this context, however, I use the term "religion" to mean the faith, the certainty, the confidence that man has in some Ultimate Ground.

When writing to the church in Rome, Paul explained that man worshipped either of two things, the true God, or some aspect of or within the created order (Rom. 1:18-23). Therefore, for some, their Ultimate Ground might be the Triune God of the Bible, for others it may be Allah the god of Islam, or the gods of the Hindu pantheon, or in reason, empiricism, etc. For a person, the Ultimate Ground serves as the foundational principle by which all of the created order can be explained. It is for this reason that Van Til, and the presuppositionalists who have followed his teaching, claim in their apologetic that "unless God is back of everything, you cannot find meaning in anything",[13] in stark contrast to the evidentialists who rarely go any deeper than the level of beliefs, and therefore never make any real progress in

---

12. Ouweneel, *Wisdom for Thinkers*, 10.
13. Cornelius Van Til, *Why I Believe in God* (Philadelphia: Committee on Christian Education of the Orthodox Presbyterian Church, n.d.), 3.

their dialogue with the unbelieving world because they have largely ignored the foundational importance of this Ultimate Ground.[14]

A person might quip that this might not apply to them because they do not identify themselves as *religious*, but an atheist is just as religious as an agnostic, and an agnostic just as religious as a Christian, because the atheist has the deep inner conviction that there is no god, just as the agnostic has the deep inner conviction that people cannot really know God, which is not altogether different from the fact that the Christian has the deep inner conviction in the God of the Bible. It is not a matter of *what* one believes, but the fact that we *do* believe. We all believe in some Ultimate Ground, in some "ultimate reality, or ultimate part or principle of reality."[15] And it is supposedly from this Ultimate Ground that we can explain the created order, that we can discern its meaning and purpose. It is what we are ultimately committed to, or to put it another way, it is the object of our heart-commitment. Now, I use the term "supposedly", not because the Ultimate Ground does not function as a foundational principle for understanding the created world, but because what that Ultimate Ground actually is for a person may not in truth succeed in providing a right and true un-

---

14. Presuppositionalism is a Christian school of thought relating to the discipline of apologetics that asserts that reasoning does not take place in a vacuum; rather, a person's reasoning is oriented by their presuppositions or assumptions, contrary to evidentialism which asserts brute (neutral, independent, isolated) facts. For more, see Greg L. Bahnsen, *Presuppositional Apologetics: Stated and Defended* (USA: American Vision, 2010).

15. Ouweneel, *Wisdom for Thinkers*, 11.

derstanding of the created world. Again, to borrow Van Til's phrase, if God is not at the back of everything, if the Triune God of the Bible is not that Ultimate Ground, then to truly *have* an understanding of the created order, along with its meaning and purpose, will be an utter impossibility.[16]

A side note needs to be made here before proceeding to a summary of all that we have covered: If someone has as their Ultimate Ground someone or something else other than the Triune God of the Bible, or the God of Christian Theism, this does not mean that they cannot know anything at all. When astronomers look up at the night sky and examine the light traveling towards us from the stars, whether they are atheists, agnostics, Christians, Muslims, etc., they can see and know that there are stars, and that their light travels towards us. Of course, they know much more than that, from the postulated composition of said stars, to the laws of physics, the rate of the speed of light, etc. We can all arrive at this knowledge, we can all *know* this, but to *truly* know this, that is to say, to truly *understand* this, is another matter. How does the astronomer make sense of the laws of physics? How does he make sense of the intelligibility of what he sees? How does he make sense of the fact that what he sees is light and not some undifferentiated data? Why are all these things intelligible to the human mind? Whatever his answers are to these questions reveals his Ultimate Ground and whether or not such an Ultimate Ground can serve as a foundational principle for understanding the created order.

---

16. See Greg L. Bahnsen, *The Impossibility of the Contrary* (Powder Springs, CA.: American Vision, 2020).

In summary, all scientific (theoretical) knowledge is rooted in a person's philosophy (or philosophical convictions), the mother of all sciences, which is in turn rooted in a person's worldview, and that worldview is rooted in a person's faith (*supra*-rational conviction), which by definition is religious in nature. I might articulate it this way: Everything from our scientific knowledge down to our worldview can be understood as "structural", while our faith can be understood as "directional". In other words, our faith determines the religious *direction* of our worldview, and thus our philosophy, and thus all our scientific (theoretical) knowledge. I have refrained from referring to our faith as "structural" because it is *supra*-rational, unlike our worldview, philosophy, and scientific (theoretical) knowledge. And that direction, that religious orientation, is either one of two: (i) vertical, if it is directed towards the Triune God of the Bible; or (ii) horizontal, if it is directed towards some aspect of or within the created order. See Figure 1. With this understanding, perhaps we can now more fully appreciate the slogan that summarized the teachings of the philosopher H. Evan Runner (1916-2002), that "life is religion."[17] As Al Wolters, who was a student of Runner, wrote: "Every aspect of human life stands in the service of either the true God of biblical religion or some substitute or idol. There is no religiously neutral ground."[18]

---

17. See H. Evan Runner, *The Collected Works of H. Evan Runner*, Vols. I-IV, ed. Kerry J. Hollingsworth and Steven R. Martins (Jordan Station, ON.: Paideia Press, 2021).

18. Al Wolters, "The Importance of H. Evan Runner", *Cardus*. Accessed September 30, 2021, https://www.cardus.ca/comment/article/the-importance-of-h-evan-runner-1/.

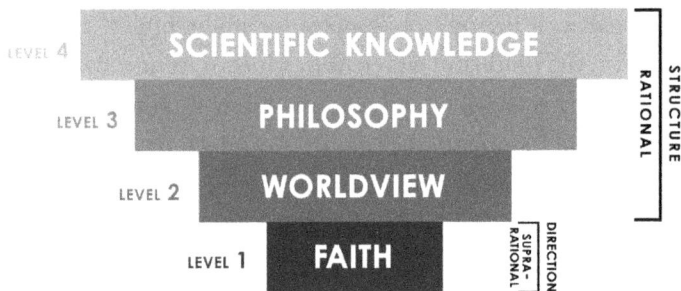

Figure 1

1.6 Returning Again to Christian Philosophy

If there is, therefore, no religiously neutral ground, and if our philosophy is rooted in our worldview, which is rooted in our faith, which is by nature religious, then there can be no such thing as a religiously *neutral* philosophy. The philosophy of the Greeks, whether or not they had the Greek pantheon as their Ultimate Ground, was religious by nature. The philosophers of past or present, in fact, are religious no matter how much they may claim to deny that fact. This is because to not be religious would be to not have faith, and therefore how could thought possibly exist without some foundational belief *for* that thought? And that then lays the groundwork for us understanding how there can actually be a *Christian* philosophy. But from the outset, it needs to be made clear that just because a philosopher claims to be a Christian does not mean that he espouses a *Christian* philosophy (think back to William Lane Craig in the Introduction), because he likely has bought into the artificial sacred-secular divide at one level or another. Even if he has endeavoured to live his whole life, that is to say, the totality of his life, in service to God, that does not mean that he has a *Christian* philosophy, because that philosophy may still be polluted by pagan syntheses (or philosophical convictions with a horizontal religious orientation). Some might think that a *Christian* philosophy can then be built upon the Bible, but as Ouweneel states, "a Christian philosophy does not mean a biblical philosophy".[19]

The Bible, as the inspired word of God, is not a science textbook, nor is it to be treated as such. To claim *Sola Scriptura* is not to claim that the Bible is to be referred to for everything in the literal sense. For example, a doctor will not turn to the Bible in order to learn how to perform heart surgery. Rather, to claim *Sola Scriptura* is to claim that the Bible is the ultimate authority for all knowledge, and so we can refer to it in this way. A doctor will then be able to turn to the Bible in order to understand his relationship to God, his relationship to his patient, and the responsibility he has, not only as a medical practitioner, but as a human being created in the image of God, for everything he does (or for every function he performs). It is because of the Bible that he can have a general understanding of the created world and His place in it. In this sense, we can understand the Bible as serving as the ultimate point of reference for our knowledge, which means that as the divinely inspired Word of God, it provides us with the parameters from which we can understand our world, or, in other words, it provides us with the building blocks for a Christian *worldview*. As Ouweneel writes:

> [The Bible] is interested in our daily matters, it speaks the language of faith. As such, it does not address the typical

---

19. Ouweneel, *Wisdom for Thinkers*, 15.

theoretical problems of science. But indirectly, through our Christian worldview, it definitely does affect the sciences, including philosophy.[20]

From where do we then get a *Christian* philosophy? From a distinctly *Christian* worldview, but you will be pleased to know that for such a theoretical enterprise we do not have to start from scratch. While we must all develop our own Christian philosophy, in the sense of learning that philosophy, we are not thrown out into the deep end of the pool to learn how to swim, there are in fact those who have gone before us who have succeeded to not only develop but also advance a *Christian* theoretical enterprise, a *Christian* philosophy. The most notable was Van Til's contemporary, the one credited with pioneering and developing a distinctly *Christian* philosophy, a *reformational* philosophy, the scholar who was regarded as "the most original philosopher Holland has produced, even Spinoza not excepted",[21] Herman Dooyeweerd (1894-1977).

---

20. Ouweneel, *Wisdom for Thinkers*, 15.
21. Prof. G.E. Langemeijer (former Attorney General of the Dutch Appeal Court and a former Chairman of the Royal Dutch Academy of Sciences – not a Christian – 1965).

2

HERMAN DOOYEWEERD, PHILOSOPHY, AND GROUND-MOTIVES

2.1 Herman Dooyeweerd

WHO IS HERMAN DOOYEWEERD (1894-1977)? There have been several books written on Dooyeweerd's life as an academic scholar and philosopher. The most comprehensive is that of Marcel Verburg, historian of the Dutch Ministry of Security and Justice, who wrote the intellectual biography *Herman Dooyeweerd: The Life and Work of a Christian Philosopher*,[1] while a significantly shortened introduction to Dooyeweerd can be found in D.F.M. Strauss' *The Philosophy of Herman Dooyeweerd*.[2] With the passing of generations, Dooyeweerd has now been more widely recognized

---

1. See Marcel E. Verburg, *Herman Dooyeweerd: The Life and Work of a Christian Philosopher* (Jordan Station, ON.: Paideia Press, 2015); Jonathan Chaplin, *Herman Dooyeweerd: Christian Philosopher of State and Civil Society* (Notre Dame, IN.: University of Notre Dame Press, 2011).

2. See D.F.M. Strauss, *The Philosophy of Herman Dooyeweerd* (Jordan Station, ON.: Paideia Press, 2021), 5-9, 107-108.

as one of the greatest Christian thinkers to have ever graced us with his presence. Dooyeweerd was a Dutch philosopher, a professor of the philosophy of law at the Free University of Amsterdam. He was born to reformed (Calvinistic) parents in Amsterdam, and given the setting and context of his upbringing, was profoundly influenced by the life and work of Abraham Kuyper (1837-1920), the Dutch theologian, statesman, and journalist. All of Dooyeweerd's translated writings into English have been published and made available by Paideia Press, part of the "Reformational Publishing Project", which seeks to publish the best works of Dooyeweerd's colleagues, students, and followers. While having written several books as part of his prolific research career, his most popular and profound works have been *The New Critique of Theoretical Thought* (originally published with the title *The Philosophy of the Law-Idea*), *In the Twilight of Western Thought*, and *Roots of Western Culture*. There are several more titles to mention, but one needs only to survey the publication catalogue of Paideia Press to appreciate all that Dooyeweerd has written. And, at the time of this writing, there are still several works in Dutch that are in the process of being translated into English.

Dooyeweerd is not the sole figure in the development of a distinct Christian philosophy, or Christian theoretical enterprise, but he is considered to be the founding philosopher in the sense that, without Dooyeweerd, we would not be here discussing such an advanced Christian philosophical system. Other notable figures, who were generally along the same lines in their thinking as Dooyeweerd, were: Dirk H.Th. Vollenhoven (1892-1978),[3] who was Dooyeweerd's

3. See Dirk H. Th. Vollenhoven, *Introduction to Philosophy*

brother-in-law and professor of philosophy at the Free University; Hendrik G. Stoker (1899-1993)[4] of Potchefstroom University (South Africa); Hendrik van Riessen (1911-2000)[5] of the Free University; Andree Troost (1916-2009)[6] of Erasmus University in Rotterdam, and H. Evan Runner (1916-2002)[7] of Calvin College (Grand Rapids, Michigan, USA). The focus of this publication will remain generally on the basics of Dooyeweerdian *Christian* philosophy. However, it should be noted that, this publication neither seeks to provide a comprehensive understanding of the complex philosophical system or to cover the *totality* of what Dooyeweerd taught. This is very much a starting point – getting one's feet wet, if you will, before diving deeper into this marvelous philosophical tradition – for the layman. For those who want to dive deeper, there are several publications to consider, such as those authored by Troost, Runner, Roy Clouser (b. 1937–),[8] and D.F.M. Strauss (b. 1946–)[9] who is

(Sioux Center, Iowa: Dordt Coll. Pr., 2005).

4. See Hendrick G. Stoker, *Conscience: Phenomena and Theories* (Notre Dame, IN.: Notre Dame University Press, 2018).

5. See Hendrik van Riessen, *The Society of the Future* (Phillipsburg, NJ.: Presbyterian and Reformed Publishing Co., 1957).

6. See Andree Troost, *What is Reformational Philosophy?: An Introduction to the Cosmonomic Philosophy of Herman Dooyeweerd* (Jordan Station, ON.: Paideia Press, 2012).

7. See H. Evan Runner, *The Collected Works of H. Evan Runner*, vols. I-IV (Jordan Station, ON.: Paideia Press, 2021).

8. See Roy A. Clouser, *Knowing with the Heart: Religious Experience and Belief in God* (USA: Wipf & Stock, 2007); *The Myth of Religious Neutrality, Revised Edition: An Essay on the Hidden Role of Religious Belief in Theories* (Notre Dame, IN.: Notre Dame University Press, 2005).

9. See D.F.M. Strauss, *Philosophy: Discipline of the Disciplines*

arguably the top Dooyeweerdian scholar alive today.

2.2 Philosophy and the Church

In the previous chapter, I had made reference to the ancient Greek philosophers as that of what we often associate in our minds with the term "philosophy", but they were not the first ones to be considered *lovers of wisdom*. That is, after all, what the term "philosophy" means, from the Greek words *philos* (friend, lover) and *sophia* (wisdom). As a philosopher had put it, "philosophy is the love of wisdom and, more importantly, the philosopher is the friend or, better, lover of wisdom."[10] As we contemplate the nature of knowledge (epistemology), and man's pursuit for knowledge (the pursuit of "wisdom"), we can discern in the world of antiquity a progression of sorts in terms of how man has gone about acquiring knowledge (wisdom): there are those whom we might call "visionaries", and then those who later succeeded them and gained prominence, the "thinkers".[11] For example, the ancient Egyptians associated the happenings of the created world with the actions of the gods, as per the creational interpretation of their priests and mystics (visionaries), and we see the same amongst the other pagan nations of antiquity (i.e., Babylon, Assyria, etc.). But there occurred a shift amongst the ancient Greeks. The Greeks were no exception,

---

(Jordan Station, ON.: Paideia Press, 2021); *Being Human in God's World* (Jordan Station, ON.: 2020).

10. Alfred J. Freddoso, "Plato (428BC-348BC)", *University of Notre Dame*. Accessed October 4, 2021, https://www3.nd.edu/~afreddos/courses/intro/platoin.htm/.

11. See Willem J. Ouweneel, *Wisdom for Thinkers: An Introduction to Christian Philosophy* (Jordan Station, ON.: Paideia Press, 2014), 17-19.

of course, given that Homer, Hesiod, etc., likewise associated the happenings of the created world with the world of the gods, but there then emerged thinkers such as Plato, Aristotle, etc., where instead of deriving their knowledge from spiritual interpretations/speculations (or from some divine medium), knowledge (or wisdom) was instead derived from man's intellect.

To put this more simply, knowledge (wisdom) was at first sought *outside* of man, but this later gave way to the pursuit of knowledge (wisdom) *within* man.[12] And yet, while we witness this progression in ancient thought, the *locus* of man's ultimate starting point is still very much himself. While the Egyptian may accredit the rising and setting of the sun with the sun-god Ra (or *Re*),[13] though he has derived this knowledge *outside* of himself (by his sight, or that of the priests/mystics), he has nonetheless *decided* that this is the correct interpretation of what he sees, so he is still very much his own epistemic authority as we later see with the Greek *thinkers*. How do we make sense of this? We could simply say that though man might have sought wisdom *outside* of himself (as a visionary) before seeking it *within* himself (as a thinker), he has nonetheless maintained his radical autonomy since the beginning, to be more specific, since the fall of man. The term "radical autonomy" can be defined as man asserting his epistemological, metaphysical/ontological, and ethical independence from the Creator God.[14] What we see

---

12. Ibid., 19.

13. Joshua J. Mark, "Ra", *World History*. Accessed October 4, 2021, https://www.worldhistory.org/Ra_(Egyptian_God)/.

14. Greg L. Bahnsen, *Van Til's Apologetic: Readings & Analysis* (Phillipsburg, NJ.: P&R Publishing, 1998), 1.

in this progression is a more pronounced autonomy, or a better aligned consistence of man's living and thinking with his pretended autonomy, in which by adopting himself as the ultimate starting point for all knowledge (and not merely the immediate starting point) he asserts his belief in the lie that he can be like God in a manner improper for a creature.

Where was true knowledge (wisdom) to be sought? That is a good question, and one which we ought to still be asking today. The ultimate starting point for all thinking must be the Creator God, the Triune God, the God of Christian theism. We will never be able to *truly* understand anything unless we presuppose Him as at the back of everything. And in order to do this, we need a worldview that is aligned with God's unified revelation, that is to say, God's creational revelation (His revelation through His creation) and God's special revelation (His revelation through His inspired Word), the latter of which serves as the authoritative interpretation of the first.[15] In God's special revelation, we learn of God as a Law-Giver, and as we view and interpret God's creational revelation through this lens, we can see and discern how this corresponds with the creational order, in the sense that there is a law-order (or "world-order"). It is because of this understanding, this *supra*-rational faith in the true God, that the sixteenth- and seventeenth-century scientific pioneers, such as Nicolaus Copernicus, Johannes Kepler, Galileo Galilei, Isaac Newton, etc., were able to make great strides in the natural sciences.[16] They understood that because there was

15. For more on this see Cornelius Van Til, *An Introduction to Systematic Theology: Prolegomena and the Doctrines of Revelation, Scripture, and God*, ed. William Edgar (Phillipsburg, NJ.: P&R Publishing, 2007).

16. Ouweneel, *Wisdom for Thinkers*, 20.; See also Henry Morris,

a law-order (world-order) to creation, and thus the causes *behind* creational (or cosmic) phenomena must be within that same creational (cosmic) reality. Not only was this concluded logically, it is also the fruit of realizing our biblical mandate, as scholar Henry Morris writes:

> …authorization for the development of science and technology was specifically commissioned in God's primeval mandate to Adam and Eve (Gen. 1:26-29), and many early scientists, especially in England and America, viewed it in just this way.[17]

Of course, we can see how the approach to finding causes behind creational (cosmic) phenomena within the same creational (cosmic) reality has been abused by naturalistic scientists today. Naturalists seek out the origin of life in every nook and cranny in this creational (cosmic) reality as opposed to in God, but the aforementioned Christian scientific pioneers differed in that they were convinced that since creation was God's handiwork, then creation must provide the answers "about what *regularities* God had placed within it."[18] They were very much engaged and more concerned with *observational* science, not *historical* science, and these terms are not in reference to any specific discipline (science) but in terms of the two *kinds* of science.[19]

Men of Science, Men of God: Great Scientists Who Believed the Bible (USA: New Leaf Press, 2020).

17. Morris, *Men of Science, Men of God*, 13-14.

18. Ouweneel, *Wisdom for Thinkers*, 20 (italicism own).

19. "There are two different *kinds* of science; observational and historical. Historical science deals with the past and is not directly testable or observable so it must be interpreted according to your worldview" (italicism own), AiG,

Returning to the question at hand, the answer is that knowledge (wisdom) is not to be sought outside of man *within creation*, nor inside of man, for he is a *creature* himself, but in the only being who is neither created nor constrained by the law-order (world-order) of creation, God. And as we come to understand God as the source of all knowledge and wisdom, and embrace Him as our ultimate epistemic starting point, it is only then that we can rightly reason (or think) and arrive at true knowledge. We see here, then, a complement of the way of "the visionary" and that of "the thinker" in terms of how man acquires true knowledge,[20] in that by receiving divine revelation from God, and basing our faith in that divine revelation (upon which we build our worldview), we are able to rightly think, philosophize, and do "science." Of course, for those who are either well-acquainted with the history of the church, or at the very least with the Christian's struggle with the noetic effects of sin,[21] the history of Christian thought has not reflected this process. Instead, what we see is a struggle between the

---

"Science", *Answers in Genesis*. Accessed October 4, 2021, https://answersingenesis.org/science/.

20. Ouweneel, *Wisdom for Thinkers*, 21.

21. The "noetic effects of sin" can be defined as "the affect sin has on the mind of every person. Sin impacts our ability to think rationally, especially about God", Steven R. Cook, "The Noetic Effects of Sin", *Thinking on Scripture*. Accessed October 4, 2021, https://thinkingonscripture.com/2017/09/17/the-noetic-effects-of-sin/. While the regenerated Christian is given a renewed mind in Christ (Rom. 12:2), we are still prone to running back to our fallen way of thinking, this includes adopting the intellectual framework of this fallen world which asserts man's sinful radical autonomy, which is why Paul exhorts the church to be actively "renew*ing*" the mind.

way of the visionary and the way of the thinker, as the scholar Ouweneel excellently explains:

> Time and again, people arose who wanted to save biblical wisdom from the claws of worldly science and fell back upon the way of seeing only [the visionary]. Or people arose who wanted to save science from the claws of rigid biblical tradition by resorting to the way of thinking only [the thinker].[22]

What might be some examples? St. Augustine (354-430 AD), for one, anticipated the pagan influence that Greek philosophy would have upon the church, and for this reason he believed that theology was the "true philosophy",[23] but this was a confusion of the two sciences (disciplines); while theology could answer *theological* questions, it could not answer *philosophical* questions.[24] However, in spite of his error, Augustine was right in discerning the religious nature of Greek philosophical thought, and it is here that we find where the Christian thinker Cornelius Van Til found support in the patristics for his Christian apologetic. If we hope to arrive at any true knowledge, if we hope to *truly* understand, as Augustine taught, we must first believe in God: "*Crede ut intelligas*" ("I believe so that I may understand"). Faith precedes understanding.

Unfortunately, this Augustinian tradition (and biblical understanding) did not persist in Christian thought as we witness later in church history. What began to gain prom-

---

22. Ouweneel, *Wisdom for Thinkers*, 21.
23. See Alfred Weber, "The Philosophy of St. Augustine", *Sophia Project: Philosophy Archives*. Accessed October 7, 2021, http://www.sophia-project.org/uploads/1/3/9/5/13955288/weber_augustine.pdf
24. Ouweneel, *Wisdom for Thinkers*, 22.

inence was the adoption of the supposed autonomous, or religiously neutral, philosophical thought, and this is best exemplified in the medieval scholastic Thomas Aquinas (1225-1274 AD). Where Augustine failed, Aquinas succeeded, in distinguishing "philosophy" and "theology" as two distinct sciences (disciplines); however, Aquinas failed where Augustine succeeded, in adopting that which was antithetical to the truth, namely, "autonomous reason".[25] What developed here was a *dualism* which we shall re-visit, a dualism between that which was considered sacred (theology) and that which was natural (philosophy).[26] Of course, while Aquinas sought to nonetheless keep both philosophy and theology together in some form, as two sciences (disciplines) walking by the hand under the same God, the resulting dualism, and the presupposition of man's autonomous reason, inevitably led to a complete divorce of the two. As Ouweneel recounts:

> ...a later thinker, William of Occam (1285-1349 AD), considered this to be hopeless. He severed theology entirely from philosophy, rejected the notion of natural theology with its so-called proofs for the existence of God, and kept divine revelation and human reason entirely separate.[27]

Not all was lost, however, as we later see in the protestant reformation a re-discovery of the all-encompassing authority of the Word of God, or to put it another way, that every aspect of creational (cosmic) existence is subject *to* God.

25. Ouweneel, *Wisdom for Thinkers*, 23.
26. See Steven R. Martins, *Apologetics: Studies in Biblical Apologetics for a Christian Worldview* (Jordan Station, ON.: Cántaro Publications, 2021), 90-93.
27. Ouweneel, *Wisdom for Thinkers*, 23.

Martin Luther (1483-1546), John Calvin (1509-1549), and even William Tyndale (1494-1536), three well-known protestant reformers amongst many, were instrumental in dismissing the notion that philosophical thought could be autonomous, or that any aspect of man could be religiously neutral. Tyndale, in particular, who is not often referred to in this realm of discussion, commented on the uselessness of the scholastic tools which were taught to him for his preparation to study and learn the Bible. Tyndale rejected these scholastic tools (or manner of thinking) as pagan and antithetical to the clear teaching of Scripture, and this further fed his growing conviction to translate the divinely inspired Scriptures into the common English tongue of his time.[28] Unfortunately, while the notion of autonomous reason was being thrown out the front door, it was being snuck back in from the back door by the likes of Philipp Melanchthon (1497-1560) and Theodore Beza (1519-1605).[29] It should be of no surprise then that autonomous reason was again upheld by many Christian thinkers, particularly during the period of the Enlightenment (18th century) – think, for example, of Immanuel Kant (1724-1804) who assigned all natural life to the realm of pure reason (rationalism)[30] – as Ouweneel again recounts:

> Many of the Enlightenment thinkers allowed God and religion their own little place – but only within the domain of re-

---

28. William Tyndale, "Practice of Prelates", in *Expositions and Notes on Sundry Portions of the Holy Scriptures together with the Practice of Prelates*, ed. H. Walker (1849; repr., Cambridge: Cambridge University Press, 1968), 291.
29. Ouweneel, *Wisdom for Thinkers*, 24.
30. John M. Frame, *A History of Western Philosophy and Theology* (Phillipsburg, NJ.: P&R Publishing, 2015), 251-270.

ligious life, the life of prayer, praise, and preaching. From the domain of philosophy, from the special sciences, and from societal life, religion was banned forever. This is what we call secularization.[31]

But while we witness still today this on-going process of *secularization,* the disassociation (or purging) of all public life from religion,[32] rationalism has been suffering a slow death ever since the disillusionment that followed the Great World Wars, the establishment of communism, the terrorist attack of 9/11, amongst other major historic events. Time has shown mankind to be much more than a *purely* rational creature, he is led by "feelings, memories, prejudices, unconscious drives and instincts" over which he has no control.[33] You could say that as we have witnessed the slow death of rationalism in modernity, what we are left with are the effects of a growing nihilism, of an existential crisis, where man can no longer know what *is* anymore, or who *he* is. And in a culture as degenerate as the West has become, we are witnessing the inevitable decay and collapse of all that we thought we knew. Dysphoria has set in while the West has dismissed the creational understanding of marriage, the family, sex, personhood, amongst a plethora of other things, all in a vain attempt to recreate the world and to acquire *true* knowledge that seemed so evasive for the natural, sinful man. However, irregardless as to man's attempt, whether individually or societally, to re-invent the world, he cannot actually re-define anything. Mankind still lives and breathes

---

31   Ouweneel, *Wisdom for Thinkers,* 24.

32. See Andrew Copson, *Secularism: Politics, Religion, and Freedom* (UK.: Oxford University Press, 2017).

33. Ouweneel, *Wisdom for Thinkers,* 25.

in God's world, and whatever he props up as an illusion will remain just that.

2.3 Religious Ground-Motives

In spite of the declining intellectual climate of the West, however, and the on-going religious prostitution of many Christians with fallen philosophical systems, God has raised up men such as Dooyeweerd, Vollenhoven, Troost, Runner, etc., men who have taken up the spirit of the reformers, to develop for the first time, beginning with Dooyeweerd, a distinctly *Christian*, reformational philosophy. A philosophy which, I would add, pays tribute to the scope and extent of the Lordship of Jesus Christ. And to illustrate just how vital Dooyeweerd was to the development of this philosophy, the Brazilian philosopher Ricardo Quadros Gouvêa writes:

> …without Dooyeweerd there would have been no reformational philosophy, and the fragmentation of the other thinkers cited would be inevitable. Dooyeweerd developed a philosophy that historically served as the unifying pole of the philosophical thought of people engaged in the Reformed or Calvinist tradition.[34]

Just as Van Til concluded against the religious neutrality of man's presuppositions in his pursuit of a *Christian* apologetic, Dooyeweerd concluded against the religious neutrality of the sciences in his pursuit of a *Christian* philosophy. And to assist us in our understanding as to what governed the minds of the philosophers, as to what were their underlying religious motivations (or direction), beginning as early

---

34. Ricardo Quadros Gouvêa, *O lado bom do calvinismo: Ensayos acerca de um calvinismo saudável* (São Paolo, Brazil: Fonte Editorial, 2013), 222.

as the ancient Greeks, Dooyeweerd proposed the *religious ground-motives* in his book *Roots of Western Culture*, of which there are four:

1) Matter-Form (the Greeks)
2) Nature-Grace (the Scholastics)
3) Nature-Freedom (the Enlightenment to the present)
4) Creation, Fall, and Redemption

The term "religious ground-motive" can be understood as the basic (*ground*) motivation (*motive*) that underlies all that we think and do.

For the ancient Greeks, their religious ground-motive was their matter-form schematic (or framework) which was articulated by their philosophers, most especially Aristotle. While it was Plato who first taught that, far above this world of fleeting things, "there was a higher world of abiding truth",[35] it was Aristotle who more fully articulated this as the matter plane (the material world) and the forms plane (the higher world of forms).[36] In brief, this world of *matter*, which we live in, is modeled after the world of the *forms*, but it becomes apparent that this world of matter is resistant to being "formed", and thus what results is an irreconcilable

---

35. Justo L. Gonzalez, *The Story of Christianity: Vol. 1: The Early Church to the Dawn of the Reformation* (USA.: HarperOne, 2014), 22.

36. For what preceded the matter-form scheme, Dooyeweerd finds roots stretching back to the ancient religious beliefs surrounding the fluid cycle of life and the rule of fate, which was set up against the Olympian gods, for more on this see Herman Dooyeweerd, *Roots of Western Culture: Pagan, Secular and Christian Options* (Jordan Station, ON.: Paideia Press, 2012).

dualism between these two planes (or storeys) of reality. This matter-form scheme (or framework) governed the thinking of the ancient Greek philosophers.

When we arrive at the medieval scholastics, however, what we see is an attempted synthesis between two antithetical worldviews, that of Christianity and Greek cosmology, resulting in the nature-grace schematic (or framework). Aquinas and Anselm could be referred to as examples, for it was Anselm who developed his theory on the "idea of God" based on the matter-form scheme of the Greeks,[37] while Aquinas is credited with facilitating the development of the nature-grace scheme. The *natural* plane (storey) consists of: natural reason (philosophy), Aristotle, the matter-form scheme, the natural world, and the institution of the state. The *grace* (that which is sacred) plane (storey) consists of God's revelation, faith, Scripture, eternal life, salvation and the church. To cite the Christian theologian and philosopher John M. Frame:

> What the [nature-grace] scheme does is take the Greek form-and-matter distinction and place that into the lower level, supplementing it with an upper level described by the term *grace*.[38]

To put it simply, the Christian could quite simply take Greek thought "pretty much as it was", treating natural philosophy as a supplement to God's revelation. What it produced, however, was another irreconcilable dualism between the nature and grace planes. To summarize what this en-

---

37 Justo L. Gonzalez, *The Story of Christianity: Vol. 1*, 378.

38. John M. Frame, *A History of Western Philosophy and Theology*, 145.

tailed, we can turn to Frame again: "On this view, Aristotle is generally sufficient to teach us about earthly matters. But to learn of heaven, we need a word from God."[39] This nature-grace scheme (or framework) was what governed the thinking of the medieval scholastics and persisted as far as the Protestant reformation and the Catholic counter-reformation. While not largely prominent today, this dualism persists in protestant circles in the form of Two Kingdoms theology, articulated by David VanDrunen in his books *Living in God's Two Kingdoms* and *Natural Law and the Two Kingdoms*.[40]

Of course, with the gradual decline of the church's political dominance over the years, and the polarizing tension produced by the nature-grace scheme, another synthesis came to take its place by means of the process of secularization. It first began with eighteenth-century Enlightenment philosophy, where we witness the elevation of *nature* to the higher plane, which can be identified as the deterministic universe of the natural philosophers, while the lower plane is the human quest for absolute *freedom*, which was the ideal of Romanticism. This nature-freedom scheme is also dualistic in nature, with the two planes proving to be irreconcilable as demonstrated by the struggles of modernist philosophers in retaining human freedom against the deterministic nature of the universe (or put more simply, the universe as a machine). This ground-motive, according to Dooyeweerd, is not only considered to have governed the philosophers

---

39. Ibid.
40. See also Willem J. Ouweneel, *The World is Christ's: A Critique of Two Kingdoms Theology* (Grimsby, ON.: Paideia Press, 2017).

of the Enlightenment, but governs still today the various "modernist" philosophers.[41]

Last is the Creation, Fall, and Redemption scheme (or framework), which is not dualistic but *ternary*, meaning consisting of three parts.[42] In this scheme there are three periods of radical creational (cosmic) change: Creation, Fall, and Redemption, all understood within the context of the Judeao-Christian worldview. This philosophical scheme introduced and developed by Dooyeweerd is thoroughly *Christian* because it does not borrow from any of the previous schemes, nor does it adopt any absolutization of some creational aspect, which renders all other religious ground-motives as idolatrous.[43] It emphasizes the undeniable conviction of the foundational significance and importance of the biblical metanarrative for understanding reality, affirming the *necessity* of God's special revelation. While this Creation, Fall, Redemption scheme is credited to Dooyeweerd, the Dutch philosopher himself credits this development to the Protestant Reformation's re-discovery of the Creation, Fall, Redemption religious ground-motive and

---

41. See Dooyeweerd, *Roots of Western Culture.*

42. "The threefold ground motive of the Word is an indivisible unity. When one slights the integral character of the creation motive, the radical sense of fall and redemption becomes incomprehensible. Likewise, whoever tampers with the radical meaning of fall and redemption cannot experience the full power and scope of the creation motive" in Dooyeweerd, *Roots of Western Culture*, 110.

43. "We absolutize an aspect of reality when we try to elevate that aspect of meaning to the totality of meaning. This is the source of all -isms in theoretical thought" in J. Glenn Friesen, "Absolutize", *Christian Nondualism*. Accessed October 7, 2021, https://jgfriesen.wordpress.com/glossary/absolutize/.

Abraham Kuyper's restoration of this ground-motive to its rightful place within Christian thought for the development of a distinctly Christian worldview and subsequent philosophy.

Altogether these four ground-motives can be further simplified into two:

1) Anastatic
2) Apostatic

When we refer to the *anastatic* ground-motive, we refer to the true *Christian* ground-motive, the ground-motive of the regenerated heart of the believer, which is the result of the work accomplished solely by the Holy Spirit. But when we refer to the *apostatic* ground-motive, we refer to the ground-motive of the unregenerate, those who are still lost in their sin, those who are essentially in "apostasy".[44] In fact, that is what the term *apostatic* means, it is the "standing out of the coherence of time because of absolutization [idolatry]", this is how Dooyeweerd regards apostasy (or apo-stasis).[45] While the term *anastatic* means "to stand again", from the term "anastasis" meaning "resurrection". Dooyeweerd uses this term "anastasis" in contrast to the term "apostasy". Put differently, we could say "anastasis" is "standing in the truth."[46] As the Dooyeweerdian philosopher J. Glenn Friesen writes, "Anastasis is therefore a re-discovering of our

---

44. Ouweneel, *Wisdom for Thinkers*, 35.
45. J. Glenn Friesen, "Anastasis", *Christian Nondualism*. Accessed October 7, 2021, https://jgfriesen.wordpress.com/glossary/anastasis/.
46 Ibid.

true self, which was lost in the fall. This is life instead of death."[47]

Understanding then *who* Dooyeweerd is, *what* his philosophic work meant in terms of its significance, *why* there was a need for a distinctly Christian philosophy – most especially after the convoluted mess of historic Christian (and worldly) thought –, and understanding the concept and schemes of *religious ground-motives*, we are now forced to ask a follow-up question: What is a distinctly *Christian* view of creational (cosmic) reality?

---

47   Ibid.

3

CREATIONAL REALITY, SPHERE SOVEREIGNTY, AND MODAL ASPECTS

3.1 Creational Reality

WHAT IS A DISTINCTLY *Christian* view of creational (cosmic) reality? What we are after is a *total* view of reality, an all comprehensive and expansive view that does not exclude anything, and thus, because of the nature of the question, a short answer cannot really be given. If I were to attempt to provide a short answer response, you would likely interpret it from your own set of presuppositions, your own pre-conceptions, and what would result is yet another synthesis of understanding created (cosmic) reality. We are not after that, we do not want to get sidetracked into another failed understanding of reality, we are pursuing a distinctly *Christian* understanding, one that is faithful to the unified (general and special) revelation of God. To arrive at this understanding, at this philosophy, we must first discard our previous way of thinking, whatever prior understanding we have of creational (cosmic) reality, in order to adopt the *Christian* view, the only *true* view through which we can make sense of created reality. Remember, there are three aspects, or components to reality: (i) metaphysics/ontology, (ii) epistemology, and (iii) ethics. From hereon forward, I will no longer refer to these as philosophical aspects, but components, in order to not cause confusion with the fifteen modal aspects of creational (cosmic) reality developed by Herman Dooyeweerd.

If philosophy consists of (i) metaphysics/ontology, (ii) epistemology, and (iii) ethics, then a *Christian* philosophy must provide us with the answer to the question: What does a Christian view of reality, knowledge, and ethics look like?[1] If you recall, from the first chapter, philosophy is not an equal science/discipline to the other special sciences/disciplines, this is because philosophy is the mother of all sciences, the discipline of the disciplines. This does not mean that the science of philosophy includes all the sciences (disciplines), because there is a distinction between a biological question and a philosophical question, there is a distinction between philosophy in general and the other special sciences. The distinction is that philosophy seeks to provide a general picture, or a totality view of creational (cosmic) reality, while the special sciences are in essence "specialized" according to their respective science/discipline. In other words, biology does not seek to provide a general picture of all creational (cosmic) reality, there are limits to the science (discipline) of biology, the same with physics, chemistry, etc. The special sciences are more specifically concerned with a particular part of creational (cosmic) reality, and thus their

---

1. Willem J. Ouweneel, *Wisdom for Thinkers: An Introduction to Christian Philosophy* (Jordan Station, ON.: Paideia Press, 2014), 39.

respective parameters of investigation are far narrower and more specialized than the science/discipline of philosophy.

What does the philosopher Dooyeweerd, therefore, present to us in terms of a *Christian* view of creational (cosmic) reality in his plethora of scholarly research and philosophical development? The fifteen modal aspects, but in order to understand these modal aspects, we ought to first explore what led him to develop this in the first place.

3.2 Kuyper, Dooyeweerd, and Sphere Sovereignty

As previously mentioned, Dooyeweerd was heavily influenced by Abraham Kuyper, truthfully one of the most extraordinary individuals of his time. Not only was he a journalist and politician, serving as the Prime Minister of the Netherlands from 1901 to 1905, but he was also a prolific intellectual and theologian, and founder of the Free University in Amsterdam. His work not only influenced Dooyeweerd, but other notable Christian thinkers such as Cornelius Van Til, Francis Schaeffer (1912-1984), Alvin Plantinga (b. 1932–), and Geerhardus Vos (1862-1949), to name a few,[2] and was instrumental in the development of Neo-Calvinism, defined as a "strain in the Christian tradition" which "stands in line with Augustine, Calvin, and many others; it is world-transformative, focused not only on the church, but on society at large, and is committed to the common good."[3] It was Kuyper who developed the

2. See "Abraham Kuyper: Collected Works in Public Theology", *Abraham Kuyper*. Accessed October 14, 2021, https://abrahamkuyper.com/.

3. The Neo-Calvinism Research Institute, "What is Neo-Calvinism?", *The Neo-Calvinism Research Institute*. Accessed October 13, 2021, https://www.neocalvinism.org/what-is-neocalvinism/.

theory of *sphere-sovereignty*, what would go on to influence Dooyeweerd towards incorporating the same principle in an understanding of creational (cosmic) reality.[4] According to the Kuyperian understanding of *sphere-sovereignty*, which is a social theory based on theological principles, not a single human institution could possibly claim absolute sovereignty because God is the absolute sovereign, instead, each human institution has its own sphere or domain of activity, and therefore, the state has no sovereignty over the church, nor the church over the state, nor the state over the family, nor the family over the state, and the same is true for societies (associations), the market (businesses), charities, etc.[5] To put it simply, each sphere has sovereignty over its own sphere or domain of activity.

This led to Dooyeweerd's development of the theory of modal aspects, in which each aspect is sovereign within its own sphere. This meant that no modal aspect can be sovereign over another, it cannot *rule* over another, and thus, also, no modal aspect could be reduced to another. Because each modal aspect is sovereign in and of itself, that means that each modal aspect has its own laws, laws which in turn cannot be reduced to the laws of another aspect.[6] In other words, these modal aspects and their respective laws are ir-

---

4. Ouweneel, *Wisdom for Thinkers*, 52.

5. See Lael Daniel Weinberger, "The Relationship Between Sphere Sovereignty and Subsidiarity" in *Global Perspectives on Subsidiarity*, ed. Michelle Evans and Augusto Zimmermann (London, UK.: Springer, 2014), 49-63.; See H. Evan Runner, *The Collected Works of H. Evan Runner, Vol. II: Walking in the Way of the Word* (Jordan Station, ON.: Paideia Press, 2021), 253-291.

6. Ouweneel, *Wisdom for Thinkers*, 53.

reducible. This is another matter to explore: the distinction of laws between modal aspects, but in order to not get ahead of ourselves, this chapter will maintain its focus on the modalities before proceeding to the notion of *law* in the next chapter.

3.3 Modal Aspects

What are modal aspects, or modalities? The term is derived from the Latin *modus*, which can mean "1. bound, limit; 2. manner, mode, way, method; 3. rule, rhythm, beat, measure, size", but in this particular instance, it means "a way of being."[7] Aside from the four religious ground-motives covered in the previous chapter, Dooyeweerd is also most known for his theory of modal aspects, the fifteen *modalities* or *modal law-spheres*, which can be said to be distinct ways in which (i) reality exists, (ii) has meaning, (iii) is experienced, and (iv) occurs.[8] To be more specific, Strauss explains:

> Whereas concrete (natural and social) entities correspond to the "what" question, modal aspects are accessible through the "how" question. From Latin we inherited expressions such as *modus operandi* and *modus vivendi* in which the *how* is represented by the term "modus." An aspect is therefore a specific (unique) mode of reality. In a general sense it is a *modus quo* or a *mode* [way] *of being*. It provides a framework within which everything and all processes within reality function. As an equivalent for referring to facets, aspects or functions,

---

7. Kevin D. Mahoney, "Latin Definition for: modus, modi", *Latdict*. Accessed October 13, 2021, https://latin-dictionary.net/definition/27114/modus-modi/.

8. For a more detailed understanding of the fifteen modalities, see D.F.M. Strauss, *The Philosophy of Herman Dooyeweerd* (Jordan Station, ON.: Paideia Press, 2021).

one can therefore also speak about *modalities, modal aspects,* or *modal functions.*[9]

Here is a list of the fifteen modal aspects in sequential order and arrangement:

1. Arithmetical (Numerical/Quantitative)
2. Spacial (Geometrical)
3. Kinematic (Motion)
4. Physical (Energetic)
5. Biotic
6. Psychical (Sensitive/Perceptive)
7. Analytical (Logical)
8. Historical (Formative)
9. Lingual
10. Social
11. Economic
12. Aesthetic
13. Juridical
14. Ethical
15. Pistical (Faith)

While the above list is in a descending order, most illustrative charts present this in an ascending order, depicting these modalities as higher levels of complexity the further you make your way up. See Figure 2 and Figure 3 for examples. How do we understand these fifteen modal aspects? Let us begin with the first and most foundational: arithmetical (numerical).

---

9.   Ibid., 39-40.

CREATURES SUBJECTED TO CREATIONAL LAWS

Aspects, Entities and Societal Institutions

Law-Spheres (Aspects)			Meaning-nuclei
Certitudinal ▲			certainty (to be sure)
Ethical ▲	Family	Church	love/troth
Juridical ▲		State	retribution
Aesthetical			beautiful harmony
Economical ▲			frugality/avoid excesses
Social	Business		social intercourse
Sign-mode			symbolical signification
Cultural-historical ▾			formative power/control
Logical			analysis
Sensitive-psychical			sensitivity/feeling
Biotical			organic life
Physical			energy-operation
Kinematic			unif. motion/constancy
Spatial			continuous extension
Numerical			discrete quantity

HUMAN & BEINGS
SOCIAL LIFEFORMS & CULTURAL THINGS

ANIMALS PLANTS THINGS

▾ Foundational function of church, state and business

▲ Qualifying function

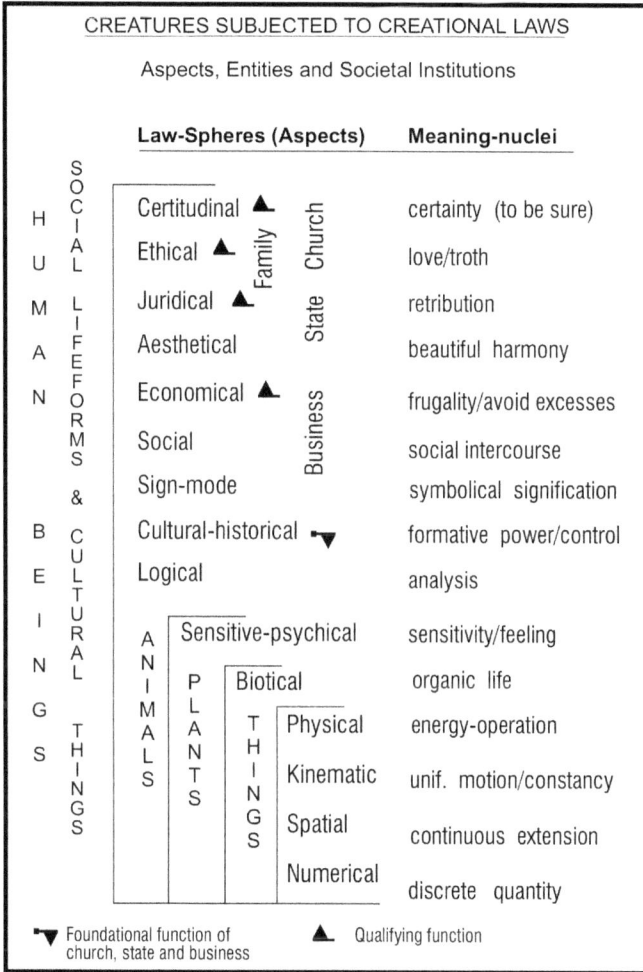

Figure 2: Source: D.F.M. Strauss, *Being Human in God's World* (Jordan Station, ON.: Paideia Press, 2020), 155.

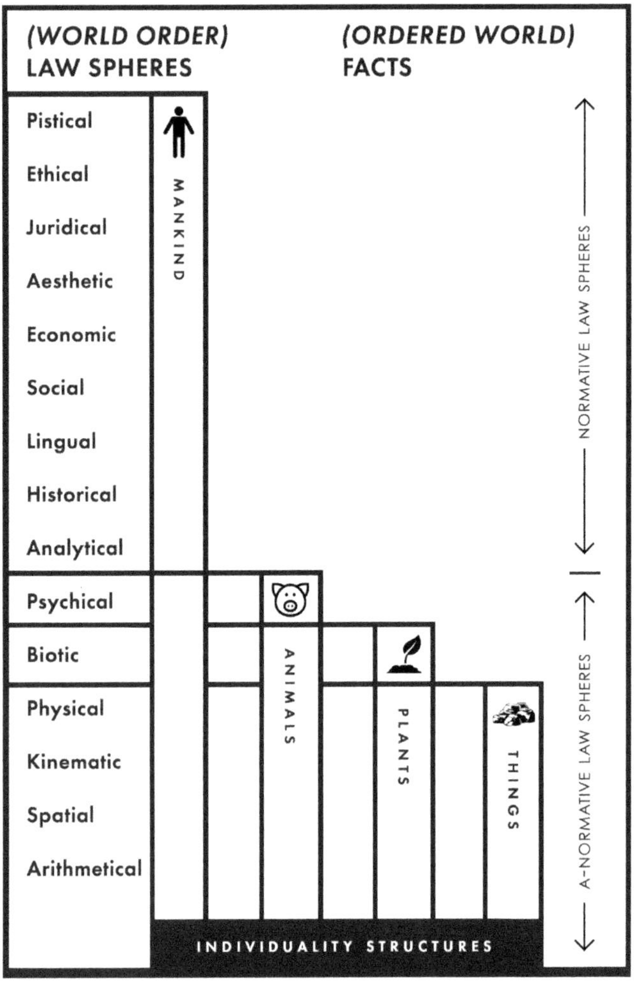

Figure 3

The arithmetical modal aspect can sometimes be referred to as the numerical or quantitative. What ought to come to mind here is the special science of mathematics, and this is why we consider the arithmetical to be foundational, because mathematics is foundational given that it is not dependent on any other special science.[10] When we speak about the mathematical, however, we do not only refer to the arithmetical (numerical/quantitative, "the one, several and many, and comparisons of less and more"[11]), but the spacial (geometrical, the "here, there, between, around, inside and outside"[12]) as well, and when determining which should be the first modality of these two, we can determine this order and arrangement based on what presupposes what. The spatial (geometrical) presupposes the arithmetical (numerical/quantitative), but the arithmetical (numerical/quantitative) does not presuppose the spatial (geometrical). For this reason the arithmetical is first, followed by the spatial as the second modality.

Then we proceed to the third modality, the kinematic (motion). When we talk about the kinematic (motion), we refer to the special science of physics, and as to why that is, as we work our way up the modality scale, Ouweneel writes that there ought to be nothing "coming in between mathematics and physics."[13] Similar to how there were two different sciences within mathematics (arithmetic and geometric), so too do we find two in physics: kinematics (motion or movement) and the physical (energy + mass, forces[14]).

10. Ouweneel, *Wisdom for Thinkers*, 40.
11. Andrew Basden, ed., "The Quantitative Aspect", *The Dooyeweerd Pages*. Accessed October 14, 2021, http://dooy.info/quantitative.html/.
12. Basden, ed., "The Spacial Aspect", *The Dooyeweerd Pages*. Accessed October 14, 2021, http://dooy.info/spatial.html/.
13. Ouweneel, *Wisdom for Thinkers*, 40.
14. Basden, ed., "The Physical Aspect", *The Dooyeweerd Pages*. Accessed October 14, 2021, http://dooy.info/physical.html/.

We know that the kinematic presupposes the spatial and arithmetical, and so for this reason it is third on the modality scale, and the reason it is not fourth is because it does not presuppose the physical (energetic), while the physical (energetic) does presuppose the kinematic (motion).

Then follows the fifth modality, the biotic (life functions + organisms[15]), and as the term implies, the biotic has to do with the special science of biology, which presupposes the physical (energetic). You can already begin to see how the modality scale progresses in complexity, with each modality presupposing what comes before it without being reduced to it. And then the sixth modality is the psychical (sensitive/perceptive), which brings us to the special science of psychology. While Ouweneel, in his *Wisdom for Thinkers: Introduction to Christian Philosophy*, argues for the breaking up of the special science of psychology into two sciences (sensations and perceptions) and therefore into two modal aspects, this diverges away from the Dooyeweerdian fifteen modality scale by positing instead sixteen modalities.[16] To maintain consistency with Dooyeweerdian philosophy, and the scholars who espouse it, we will remain with the original fifteen modal law-spheres.

What follows after the psychical modal aspect? The analytical (logical) aspect, which brings us into the humanities, those special sciences that examine human phenomena. How does the analytical (logical) presuppose the psychical and the biotic? Well, the analytical (logical) cannot do without a mind (psychical), and without a brain (biotic), hence

---

15. Basden, ed., "The Biotic Aspect", *The Dooyeweerd Pages*. Accessed October 14, 2021, http://dooy.info/biotic.html/.

16. Ouweneel, *Wisdom for Thinkers*, 41.

why the analytical (logical) is the seventh modality because it presupposes all the modalities that come before it. And what follows this in sequential order and arrangement is the historical (formative) modal aspect, which concerns, of course, the science of historiography, and being the eighth modal aspect it presupposes the analytical (logical) aspect.

The ninth modal aspect is lingual (experienced as "expressing, recording and interpreting"[17]), based on the science of linguistics which examines language phenomena, and as is evident in linguistics, this science and modal aspect presupposes the historical (formative) aspect because it presupposes the "historical process."[18] Then we have the tenth modal aspect, being the social, for the science of sociology is a natural progression from linguistics, of which the social presupposes. And then the eleventh modal aspect that follows is the economic, the science of economics also progresses naturally from the sociological. Then the final four, with the twelfth modal aspect being aesthetics – and while we may think of the arts, this modal aspect goes beyond the arts and includes "harmonizing, enjoying, playing, beautifying" – ;[19] the thirteenth modal aspect being juridical, the science of jurisprudence; the fourteenth modal aspect being ethical, the science of morality; and then the fifteenth modal aspect being pistical, from the Greek word *pistis* meaning "faith", therefore the science of "pistical" phenomena which

---

17. Basden, ed., "The Lingual Aspect", *The Dooyeweerd Pages*. Accessed October 14, 2021, http://dooy.info/lingual.html/.

18. Ouweneel, *Wisdom for Thinkers*, 42.

19. Basden, ed., "The Aesthetic Aspect", *The Dooyeweerd Pages*. Accessed October 14, 2021, http://dooy.info/aesthetic.html/.

is not to be confused with the term religious.[20] Aesthetics presupposes the economical, while the economical does not presuppose aesthetics. The juridical presupposes the aesthetic, if we think about "harmony" and keeping the harmony (peace), but the aesthetic does not presuppose the juridical. The ethical (moral) presupposes the juridical, because it presupposes "justice", but the juridical does not presuppose the ethical (moral) – as strange as this might seem, when examined more closely it makes sense, for the juridical concerns "appropriateness and due",[21] while ethics concerns "attitude, self-giving love" which includes an element of "vulnerability and sacrifice" – in other words, in the ethical function, we go beyond what is due, "giving more than necessary, even at expense to ourselves."[22] And the pistical (faith) presupposes the ethical and not the other way around, for the pistical concerns "aspiration, commitment, certainty and belief."[23]

This may seem rather complex, but as should be expected of a philosophy that seeks to provide a *totality* view of creational reality, it must be given that this world is incredibly complex. Nonetheless we can still make some progress in understanding how this modal scale works. If we were to ask, for example, how can this modality scale be applied? Well, for that, we can look at an illustration provided by Strauss in his book *Being Human in God's World*:

---

20. Ouweneel, *Wisdom for Thinkers*, 43.
21. Basden, ed., "The Juridical Aspect", *The Dooyeweerd Pages*. Accessed October 14, 2021, http://dooy.info/juridical.html/.
22. Basden, ed., "The Ethical Aspect", *The Dooyeweerd Pages*. Accessed October 14, 2021, http://dooy.info/ethical.html/.
23. Basden, ed., "The Pistical Aspect", *The Dooyeweerd Pages*. Accessed October 14, 2021, http://dooy.info/pistic.html/.

...a chair possesses four legs (numerical: the interest of mathematical arithmetic); it is large or small (spatial aspect; mathematical geometry); is a wheelchair or not (movement aspect: kinematic); it is strong or weak (physical-chemical aspect); it is usable in human life (although as biotic object because a chair has no life – biology studies reality from the biotic aspect); it is comfortable (sensitive-psychic aspect: psychology); it is identifiable and distinguishable (analytical aspect: logic); it is culturally formed (historical aspect: historical science would be interested in, for instance, the historical development of different chair styles); it has a name (a verbal sign – the sign aspect; general semiotics and linguistics); it is used in the interaction of people (social aspect: sociology); it has a price (economic aspect: economics); it is beautiful or ugly (aesthetic aspect: aesthetics); it belongs to someone who has a subjective right to it (a competence to dispose and enjoy it – juridical aspect: legal science); it is or isn't someone's favourite seat (ethical/love aspect: ethics); and it is reliable – everyone believes that the chair will carry them if they sit on it (faith aspect: viewpoint of theology as science)... Such trust [faith aspect] must not be confused with trusting faith in the religious sense – except of course if someone were to make an idol of the particular chair![24]

While I have taken the time and space here to explain the modal aspects and their sequential order and arrangement, there is still *a lot* to be said regarding the general structure of modal aspects, such as their law-side/norm-side, the factual side, the time-order, the time-duration, the subject-subject and subject-object relations, and much more.[25]

---

24. D.F.M. Strauss, *Being Human in God's World* (Jordan Station, ON.: Paideia Press, 2020), 127-128.

25. See Strauss, *The Philosophy of Herman Dooyeweerd*, 47-48.;

While I will address the law side of created reality to some extent in the next chapter, for most of this more *profound* understanding of modal aspects, I must hand that off to the more specialized Dooyeweerdian philosophers, and thankfully there are plenty to turn to, whether that be D.F.M. Strauss, Andree Troost, Roy A. Clouser, etc. A special mention, however, needs to be made of Joseph Boot with the Ezra Institute, who is a rising Christian thinker, not only known for his Van Tillian apologetic, but for his masterful handling of the contours of Dooyeweerdian Christian philosophy.[26] Any reader wishing to acquaint himself (or herself) with a distinctly Christian philosophy would benefit greatly from reading his works and listening to his lectures. All of this I write to simply say that, what I have written here is merely an *introduction* and a *starting point* for the development of our own (personal) Christian understanding of created reality.

But that provokes the question, What makes this modality scale a *Christian* understanding of reality? I will do my best to answer that question, but first I must clarify what these modal aspects are.

3.4 Religious Direction

The fifteen modalities developed and presented by Dooyeweerd can be understood as fifteen "windows through which we can look at cosmic reality", these aspects have an "epis-

Basden, ed., "Dooyeweerd's Suite of Modal Aspects", *The Dooyeweerd Pages*. Accessed October 13, 2021, http://dooy.info/aspects.to1005.html/.

26. See, for example, Joe Boot, "Recovering the Christian Mind" in *Jubilee: Recovering Biblical Foundations for our Time* (Grimsby, ON.: Ezra Press, Summer 2019).

temological character", as well as an "ontological character", but here I must add another, they also have an *ethical character* in terms of how man treats these modalities. We must remember that all of life is religion, that man is an inescapably religious being, and as a result, all that he does and thinks is either directionally oriented vertically in worship of the Creator God, or horizontally in idolatrous worship of creation. What makes these fifteen modalities a *Christian* understanding of reality is that in place of absolutizing one of the modalities or reducing all of created reality into a single modality in order to arrive at a true understanding of creational (cosmic) reality, we instead reduce all things into the single principle of their origin, which is the Creator God of general and special revelation, the God of Christian theism. This is not a *monistic* understanding of reality, because we hold to a Creator-creation distinction, and this is also not a *dualistic* understanding of reality because we do not hold to two irreconcilable principles. The unregenerate heart, however, will absolutize one of the modalities, or some aspect of creation, in order to arrive at an understanding of creational (cosmic) reality, but not only does this method fail in its attempt to make sense of reality (the process of predication), it also commits the sin of idolatry by substituting the Creator God at the back of everything with some creational aspect (Cf. Rom. 1:21-23). What might be an example of this? Stephen Hawking (1942-2018), the celebrated English theoretical physicist and cosmologist believed and dedicated his life's work towards finding the mathematical formula (or equation) that would explain all of life,[27] of course, the more

---

27. See Stephen Hawking, *A Brief History of Time* (New York, NY.: Bantam, 1998).

he progressed in his pursuit, the more aware he became that such a possibility was an impossibility.[28] We cannot reduce the modal aspects, they are irreducible, and we cannot absolutize any creational aspect. If we seek to truly understand creational (cosmic) reality, we must turn to the God of heaven and earth.

In conclusion, since the theoretical concept of modal aspects put forward by Dooyeweerd is very much new to the modern thinker, I cite Ouweneel to help further simplify what these aspects are and what they are not:

> …modal aspects are not themselves phenomena but always only *aspects* of phenomena. Aspects are ways things are (to put it ontologically): they are arithmetical, spatial, etc. Aspects are also ways we can view things (to put it epistemologically): they can be viewed from an arithmetical angle, a geometrical angle, etc.[29]

I would add one more thing: Aspects are also ways we understand things as being rightly directionally oriented in worship (to put it ethically) towards God, or wrongly towards creation. We ought to remind ourselves that worship has an ethical character to it, it is either righteous in its worship of the true God, or sinful in its idolatrous worship of creation. All that we do, whether in public or in private, is done *Coram Deo*, Latin for "in the presence of God."

---

28. Stephen Hawking, "Gödel and the End of Physics: Stephen Hawking", *The Pickett Group*. Accessed October 14, 2021, http://yclept.ucdavis.edu/course/215c.S17/TEX/GodelAndEndOfPhysics.pdf

29. Ouweneel, *Wisdom for Thinkers*, 51.

4

GOD, CREATION, AND CREATIONAL LAW

4.1 Modal Aspects as Law-Spheres

THERE CAN BE NO conversation about Dooyeweerd's fifteen modalities, or modal aspects, even at a purely introductory level, without taking into consideration and discussing what Dooyeweerd meant by articulating modalities as *law-spheres*. It is by understanding the *law-side* of these modalities that we can understand how everything in creational (cosmic) reality can function in every single one of the fifteen modal aspects. The question we must now ask is, therefore: What does Dooyeweerd mean by *law-spheres*?

The development of the natural sciences came about as a result of man's discernment of creation following a fixed *law-order*, a notion that is increasingly discarded by modern intelligentsia but was vital to the pioneering work of the natural sciences. But the law-order of creation, or creational law-order, is not merely a notion, that is to say, it is not merely a theory or general idea, it is an indisputable fact given that (i) it is revealed by God's general revelation (creation); (ii) it is revealed by God's special revelation (Scripture); and (iii) it is revealed by man's living and thinking. While the third could be included within the first, that is, man's living and thinking forms a part of God's general revelation,[1] I make a distinction here because in the first I mean man's observation of creational (cosmic) reality (not including himself), and in the third, his presupposing of a fixed *law-order* in his living and thinking – the confessed beliefs of the regenerate would be consistent with the presuppositions of his living and thinking, while the beliefs of the unregenerate would be inconsistent, denying the fixed law-order as defined by the Word of God but relying on that fixed law-order in order to make that denial.[2] What does the Bible, the divinely inspired Scriptures, have to say about the law-order? Prior to answering that question, I need to again clarify that while the Bible does not teach us philosophy, in terms of the development or articulation of a theoretical enterprise, it *does* provide us with the parameters by which we can build and develop a right and true *world-and-life-view* or *worldview*. And the fixed law-order of creational (cosmic) reality is a vital, foundational component to the Christian, biblical worldview. Understanding this then, here are a few biblical passages from which we learn about the fixed law-order (again, recall that God's special revelation was given as the only authoritative interpretation of

---

1. See Cornelius Van Til, *Christian Apologetics* (Phillipsburg, NJ.: P&R Pub., 2003), 70.; Steven R. Martins, *Apologetics: Studies in Biblical Apologetics for a Christian Worldview* (Jordan Station, ON.: Cántaro Publications, 2021), 97-99.

2. For more on this, see Greg L. Bahnsen, *Pushing the Antithesis: The Apologetic Methodology of Greg L. Bahnsen* (Powder Springs, GA.: American Vision, 2007).

created reality):

> In the beginning God created the heavens and the earth (Gen. 1:1).

> Do you know the ordinances of the heavens? Can you establish their rule on the earth? (Job 38:33).

> Forever, O Lord, your word is firmly fixed in the heavens... By your appointment they stand this day, for all things are your servants (Ps. 119:89).

> And he established them forever and ever; he gave a decree, and it shall not pass away (Ps. 148:6).

> I made the earth and created man on it; it was my hands that stretched out the heavens, and I commanded all their host (Isa. 45:12).

> Thus says the Lord, who gives the sun for light by day and the fixed order of the moon and the stars for light by night, who stirs up the sea so that its waves roar – the Lord of hosts is his name: "If this fixed order departs from before me, declares the Lord, then shall the offspring of Israel cease from being a nation before me forever" (Jer. 31:35-36).

> Thus says the Lord: If I have not established my covenant with day and night and the fixed order of heaven and earth... (Jer. 33:25).

> You are the Lord, you alone. You have made heaven, the heaven of heaves, with all their host, the earth and all that is on it, the seas and all that is in them; and you preserve all of them; and the host of heaven worships you (Neh. 9:6).

> ...we bring you good news, that you should turn from these vain things to a living God, who made the heave and the earth and the sea and all that is in them (Acts 14:15).

By faith we understand that the universe was created by the word of God, so that what is seen was not made out of things that are visible (Heb. 11:3).

"Worthy are you, our Lord and God, to receive glory and honor and power, for you created all things, and by Your will they exist and came to be" (Rev. 4:11).

While there are several other instances in the Bible from which we learn about the fixed law-order of creational (cosmic) reality, the above will suffice for us to understand that (i) creational (cosmic) reality has laws, (ii) creational (cosmic) reality is subject to those laws, and (iii) those laws which govern creational (cosmic) reality are provided by a sovereign Law-Giver. Hence why Dooyeweerd originally titled his *New Critique of Theoretical Thought* as *The Philosophy of the Law Idea*.[3] In relation to our discussion of a fixed law-order, here I must make mention of two terms that are often confused together but that are actually quite different; two terms which are commonly referred to in the articulation of this Dooyeweerdian, Christian philosophy: The first is "ordered world", which means everything in creational (cosmic) reality, such as things, plants, animals, man, societies, institutions, etc. This "ordered world" is sometimes referred to as the world of "facts." But "world order" – and this is the root of the confusion, the words "order" and "world" have been swapped around – means the laws that exist and that govern all things in the "ordered world."[4] In this Chris-

---

3. See Herman Dooyeweerd, *A New Critique of Theoretical Thought*, Vols. I-IV (Jordan Station, ON.: Paideia Press, 2016).

4. Willem J. Ouweneel, *Wisdom for Thinkers: Introduction to Christian Philosophy* (Jordan Station, ON.: Jordan Station, ON., 2014), 60.

tian philosophy, or theoretical enterprise, "ordered world" is on the *factual side*, also referred to as the *subject-side*, while the "world order" is on the *law-side* of creational (cosmic) reality.[5] As we refer to the modal aspects, therefore, we can understand then that, as per scholar Willem J. Ouweneel:

> On the one hand, the aspects refer to the factual matters of which they are aspects. On the other hand, the aspects comprise certain laws that are typical of these aspects and that hold for the factual matters of *which* they are aspects... The laws govern the facts, the facts are under the laws.[6]

4.2 Factual side and Law-side

What might be some examples that could help facilitate our understanding? Let us think about the first modal aspect, the arithmetical (numerical/quantitative). Numbers (1, 2, 3, etc.) are on the factual (or subject-) side of creational (cosmic) reality, whereas the arithmetical laws of the commutative, associative, and distributive are examples of the law-side. What is the commutative law? It is the law that when we add, or multiply, the order of the numbers would not affect the outcome (i.e., $1 + 2 + 5 = 8$; $5 + 2 + 1 = 8$; $2 \times 5 = 10$; $5 \times 2 = 10$). This law does not apply, however, to subtraction or division, where the order of the numbers would affect the outcome.[7] The associative law, on the other hand, says that it does not matter how we group the num-

---

5. Ibid.
6. Ibid.
7. "Algebra Laws: Commutative, Associative, Distributive Laws", *Whatcom Community College*. Accessed October 18, 2021, https://www.whatcom.edu/home/showpublisheddocument/1702/635548016545030000/.

bers (i.e. which numbers we calculate first) when we add or multiply; and as for the distributive law, that we get the same result when we multiply a number by a group of numbers added together, or if we multiply them separately and then add them.[8] But let me further simplify my point, 1 + 1 = 2 is perhaps the first arithmetical law we learn in our lives, and while the components (numbers) are of the *factual* (subject-) side of the arithmetical modality, the law is of the *law*-side.

Let us now think about the second modal aspect, the spatial (geometrical). If I draw a square, or a circle, or a triangle, or some other shape, these shapes or figures are on the factual (or subject-) side of creational (cosmic) reality, whereas Euclid's Postulates and the Pythagorean theorem are examples of the law-side. Euclid's Postulate 1, for example, states that a straight line segment can be drawn joining any two points; Postulate 2, that any straight line segment can be extended indefinitely in a straight line, and Postulate 3, that given any straight line segment, a "circle can be drawn having the segment as radius and one endpoint as center."[9] And as for the Pythagorean Theorem, that in a right triangle, the square of the hypotenuse equals the sum of the square of the lengths of the legs, otherwise presented as $c^2 = a^2 + b^2$.[10] You can now begin to understand the *factual*

8. Commutative, Associative, and Distributive Laws", *Math is Fun*. Accessed October 18, 2021, https://www.mathsisfun.com/associative-commutative-distributive.html/.

9. "Euclid's Postulates", *Wolfram MathWorld*. Accessed October 18, 2021, https://mathworld.wolfram.com/EuclidsPostulates.html/.

10. "Pythagorean Theorem", *Wolfram MathWorld*. Accessed October 18, 2021, https://mathworld.wolfram.com/Pythagore-

(or subject-) side of the spatial modality, and the *law*-side.

And let us try another aspect, the third modal aspect, the kinematic (motion). Forward, backward, upward and downward is on the factual (or subject-) side of creational (cosmic) reality. Think of a baseball being thrown by a pitcher in a certain direction – while we could talk about the physical, let us focus on the movement of the ball in a particular direction – whereas Galileo's law of motion would be an example of the law-side. What is Galileo's law on motion? This is the law that an object moving on a frictionless horizontal plane must neither have acceleration nor retardation, i.e., it should move with constant velocity.[11] Of course, you can begin to see how this modal aspect presupposes what comes before it, the arithmetical and the spatial.[12] If you were to try to reduce this kinematic aspect to the spatial (which presupposes the arithmetical), what you would be left with is Zeno's paradox.[13] Perhaps now you have a clearer

anTheorem.html/.

11. "Galileo's thought experiment", *Institute of Physics*. Accessed October 19, 2021, https://spark.iop.org/galileos-thought-experiment/.

12. For more on the arithmetical and geometrical, and the kinematic and the physical, see D.F.M. Strauss, *The Significance of a Non-Reductionist Ontology for the Disciplines of Mathematics & Physics: A Historical & Systematic Analysis* (Jordan Station, ON.: Paideia Press, 2021).

13. See Ethan Siegle, "This is How Physics, Not Math, Finally Resolves Zeno's Famous Paradox", *Forbes*. Accessed October 18, 2021, https://www.forbes.com/sites/startswithabang/2020/05/05/this-is-how-physics-not-math-finally-resolves-zenos-famous-paradox/?sh=d4ca62a33f8f/.; See Danie F.M. Strauss "The Philosophy of the Cosmonomic Idea and the Philosophical Foundations of Mathematics", *Philosophia Reformata* (published online

picture as to why modal aspects, or modalities, are referred to as modal *law-spheres*, for as Ouweneel puts it, "Every modal aspect, or law-sphere, has its own characteristic laws that you do not find in any other aspect."[14]

4.3 Laws and Norms

There is, however, a distinction between the first to sixth modal aspects and the seventh to fifteenth in regard to the character of their laws, the first to sixth modal aspects have to do with "natural laws", whereas the seventh to fifteenth have to do with "norms". How can we understand this distinction? We can answer that question by putting it this way: The natural laws cannot be violated, 1 + 1 will always = 2, to break these natural laws would be to disqualify them as laws. Or to put it more simply, we cannot disobey natural laws, such a choice is not available to us, it is an impossibility. Norms, on the other hand, can be disobeyed. How so? While there are laws of logic, such as, for example, the law of non-contradiction, if one so desired, they could choose to violate this law (or norm) and therefore be considered illogical. A helpful way to distinguish what is law and what is norm is whether the opposites are possible, for example, the opposite of logical is illogical, the opposite of historical is ahistorical, the opposite of social is asocial, the opposite of economic is uneconomic, and etc., as you make your way up the modality scale. But you cannot say the same about the arithmetical, there is no such as the unarithmetical, or aspatial, or the unbiotic, etc., these terms do not exist in the

---

ahead of print 2021). https://doi.org/10.1163/23528230-BJA10014 Web.

14. Ouweneel, *Wisdom for Thinkers*, 61.

sense that we could violate or disobey these respective laws.[15] While it may be easy to discern what are *natural laws*, how do we discern *norms*? Natural laws tell us what *is* in our creational (cosmic) reality, whereas norms are what *ought to be* in our creational (cosmic) reality. These laws and norms find their origin in the Creator God, who placed these within creation, however, we must take great care when articulating these norms, for as Ouweneel explains, while there exists analytical (logical), historical (formative), lingual, social, economic, aesthetic, juridical, ethical, and pistical (faith) norms,

> they are not inventions of Man. At least, this is a matter that has to be constantly investigated in order to distinguish temporary, man-made norms from permanent, God-given norms... On the one hand, Christian philosophy is convinced that the natural laws and... norms identified so far have at least something to do with the nature of cosmic reality as such... On the other hand, our knowledge of these laws and norms is always preliminary, always open to criticism and to further philosophical and scientific investigation.[16]

4.4 The *Imago Dei*

As we discuss the nature of laws and norms in relation to the modal law-spheres, a note needs to be made here about the uniqueness of the human individual. In what sense? In the sense that the human individual is the only creature in creational (cosmic) reality that can disobey norms, meaning that no other living thing in creation can disobey norms. Not only that, only man can disobey norms and *feel guilty*,

15. Ibid., 63.
16. Ibid., 62-63, 65.

the inevitable result of knowing the norms and how they were violated, what some may refer to as a person's *conscience*.[17] We derive this understanding from God's special revelation, in that man is *responsible* for his own sin (Gen. 6:5; Ps. 51:5; Eccl. 7:20; Jer. 17:9; Mark 7:21; John 3:19; Rom. 3:9-19, 23; Titus 1:15-16; 2 Pet. 2:14) – though God's general revelation of creation also reveals the fallenness of creation by its appearance being as in need of redemption – but we do not see that being the case with other created creatures placed under man. Can a squirrel ever fall into sin? No. Can a chimpanzee ever fall into sin? No. And could these creatures ever feel guilt for sin? Again, no. Any living thing other than mankind cannot disobey norms, nor therefore have feelings of guilt for disobeying norms. The reason that man has a place of *responsibility* under God and over all creation, and a response to that responsibility if he fails to comply with God's creational intention, is precisely because he has the capability of abiding by or disobeying norms. Why is this the case? Because man was created in the *imago Dei*, in the image of God. As the *Baker Encyclopedia of the Bible* defines it:

> Likeness to God, the most basic affirmation to be made concerning the nature of man from a Christian perspective. Man is unique among the creatures in that he is like God and therefore able to have communion and fellowship with God.[18]

Or to put it simply, to be created in the *imago Dei* is

17. Ibid., 69.
18. N. Shepherd, "Image of God" in *Baker Encyclopedia of the Bible*, Vol. 1 (Grand Rapids, MI: Baker Book House, 1998), 1017.

to be created to be like God as much as a *creature* possibly could. Why do I emphasize the term "creature"? Because there *is* a Creator-creation distinction, this is how we can understand creational law as a *boundary* of sorts, in that God is on the outer side of the boundary (and therefore not subject to creational law), while all of creation is on the inner side of the boundary (and therefore subject to creational law). And while this boundary separates, or creates a distinction between Creator and creation, it is also the "connection point" between the Creator and creation.[19]

What happens if this Creator-creation distinction is blurred? You either elevate creation to the position of the Creator, or reduce the Creator to the position of creation, and in either case you are left with an indiscernible monistic oneness, within which no distinctions are made possible and all of reality is rendered unintelligible.[20] The Creator-creation distinction, or the boundary (law-order), is therefore necessary in order to make sense of our creational (cosmic) reality. On a theological side note, this boundary makes the divine incarnation all the more remarkable, for God the Son, who is above creational law, took on human flesh, and thus as a man, Jesus was subject to creational law. The One who is above creational law also being at the same time subject to creational law? The mystery of the hypostatic union, the "union of a perfect human nature with the eternal Logos without confusion of natures in the person of Christ", is certainly profound, but it does not make it any less true.[21]

---

19. Ouweneel, *Wisdom for Thinkers*, 74-75.
20. Van Til, *Christian Apologetics*, 30-31.; Martins, *Apologetics*, 102.
21. A. Cairns, "Hypostatic Union" in *Dictionary of Theological*

4.5 Subject and Object Functions

We shall see in the next chapter the place of man in creational (cosmic) reality in light of being created in the *imago Dei*, for his placement in creation came with a mandate, and with the help of Christian philosophy we can make significant progress toward fulfilling that mandate. But we cannot proceed any further without first surveying the subject and object functions of the fifteen modalities, because as we saw with the example provided by Strauss of the chair, without understanding the subject and object functions, we will not be able to understand how Strauss arrived at such an illustration, or whether we can come up with an illustration of our own.

We begin first with subject functions. Everything in our creational (cosmic) reality can function in all fifteen modal aspects. For example, we could refer to a tree which we know is governed by the laws of the arithmetical (numerical, quantitative), the spatial (geometrical), the kinematic (motion), the physical (energetic), and the biotic. There is no question about that. But did you know that a tree can also function in the higher aspects, such as the analytical (logical), historical (formative), or lingual aspects? You might say, however, that a tree can neither think logically, nor give form or create (in the historical-formative aspect), nor speak. This is where the subject and object distinction becomes useful. When we use the term "subject" epistemically, we mean the one who *knows*, while the term "object" means that which is around us that we may *know*. Ontologically, however, the terms "subject" and "object" help us to under-

Terms (Greenville, SC.: Ambassador Emerald Int., 2002), 218.

stand how things function.

Let us continue with our tree example. A tree functions as a subject in the first to fifth modal aspects, from the arithmetical up to the biotic. But beyond the biotic, the tree functions as an object, in what way? In the sense that they are not subject to the laws of the higher modal aspects, but they are objects in relation to man's interaction with them, and this interaction is subject to the laws of the higher modal aspects. For example, a tree may not be an analytical (logical) subject, but it can be an analytical object in that man thinks of the tree. A tree may also not be a historical (formative) subject, but it can be a historical (formative) object in that man cultivates it. It may also not be a lingual subject, but it can be a lingual object if it is given a scientific name. To put it simply, a tree has five subject-functions (arithmetical, spatial, kinematic, physical, and biotic), and it has ten object-functions (psychical, analytical, historical, lingual, social, economic, aesthetic, juridical, ethical, pistical). A note worth mentioning here, these object-functions are not activated until there is some human interaction. This should provide some clarity as to how Strauss arrived at his illustration of a chair functioning in all fifteen modal aspects, but for the case of the chair, it has four subject-functions (arithmetical, spatial, kinematic, and physical), and eleven object-functions. To provide some further clarity, it is scholar Andrew Basden who states:

> Any entity can function as object in any aspect. But not all entities can function as subject in all aspects, and the latest aspect in which an entity can function as subject defines what *kingdom* it is in. This provides a useful way of understanding

the notion of *kingdoms*... four traditional *kingdoms* of physical things, plants, animals and humans.[22]

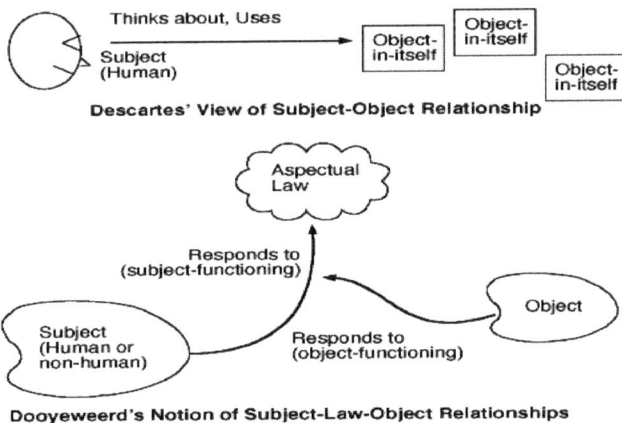

Descartes' View of Subject-Object Relationship

Dooyeweerd's Notion of Subject-Law-Object Relationships

Figure 4: Source: Steve Bishop, "Portraits: Subject-Law-Object Relationships", *All of Life Redeemed*. Accessed October 21, 2021, https://www.alloflliferedeemed.co.uk/Portraits/subjobj.jpg/.

Yes, the notion of kingdoms in Dooyeweerdian, Christian philosophy has not been introduced to you, and that is worth a whole other discussion. However, altogether, from the beginning of this book up to this current stage, all that I have done is lead you by the hand to discover and explore the surface level of this Christian philosophical system, or theoretical enterprise, conceived and developed by Dooyeweerd and his contemporaries and successors. In exception of the next and last chapter, this is as far as I bring you in this exciting journey of the development of our own personal, distinctly Christian philosophy. Whether we like it or not, we are *all* philosophers in that we *all* have preconceived beliefs and ideas as to what creational (cosmic) reality is, and it

22. Andrew Basden, "Subjects, Objects, and Things", *The Dooyeweerd Pages*. https://dooy.info/subject.object.html/.

is our responsibility as men and women created in the *imago Dei* to ensure that our worldview, and therefore the philosophy that stems from that worldview, aligns with the unified (general and special) revelation of God, so that directionally, in our religious orientation, we are giving due worship to the God of heaven and earth. To put it another way, with the book that you hold in your hands, you have merely wet your feet on the beach, but I commend you to the philosophical geniuses of past and present, such as Dooyeweerd, D. H. Th. Vollenhoven, Andree Troost, H. Evan Runner, Roy Clouser, D. F. M. Strauss, Willem J. Ouweneel, Joseph Boot, amongst others, who will not only help you swim towards the depths but to dive deep into this Christian philosophical system in our quest to know and understand truly our creational (cosmic) reality for the glory of God. As a matter of fact, there is another book worth visiting, a next step from here, one could argue, towards understanding this philosophy, compiled and edited by Strauss, and published by Paideia Press, *Dooyeweerd for Dummies.*[23]

23. See *Paideia Press*. Accessed October 20, 2021, https://paideiapress.ca/.

5

THE VITALITY
OF A CHRISTIAN
UNDERSTANDING
FOR CHRISTIAN
LIVING

5.1 The Renewal of the Mind

AFTER HAVING DIPPED our toes in the Christian philosophical system developed and introduced by the Dutch polymath[1] Herman Dooyeweerd, there remains a lingering question that we must answer if we hope to better understand its necessity for Christian living. Why do we need a Christian philosophical understanding of creational (cosmic) reality? We might think about the humble missionaries in red zones[2] who have never heard of Dooyeweerd, or who,

---

1. A person of wide-ranging knowledge or learning; Cf. Kerry J. Hollingsworth, "About", *The Reformational Digital Library*. Accessed November 3 2021, https://reformationaldl.org/about/.

2. The last frontiers, see "Red Zones: The Last Frontiers for Missions", *Modern Day*. Accessed November 3, 2021, https://www.modernday.org/red-zones-last-frontiers-missions/.

perhaps, have never read a book written by or about Plato, or Aristotle; or maybe we might think about the Christians in third-world countries who think more about their everyday needs, such as what they will eat and drink, and who have neither the luxury nor the time to be contemplating such things. If they have been able to manage *without* a Christian philosophy all this time, then why do we need one at all?

To answer that question, I turn our attention to the words of the apostle Paul written to the church in Rome in the first century AD: "Do not conform to the pattern of this world, but be transformed by the renewing of your mind. Then you will be able to test and approve what God's will is – his good, pleasing and perfect will" (Rom. 12:2). We will first consider the meaning of the first half of the verse before moving on to the second. When Paul writes "do not conform to the pattern of this world", he means not to live according to the world of the passing age, meaning the fallen world that is being done away with and which is giving up its place to the redeemed creation. Thus, Christians are to "live for God and not be conformed to any other standard", or way of living, as per commentator J.A. Fitzmyer.[3] And this non-conformism is achieved by the *transforming* of our minds, the "metamorphosis" of our "thinking, willing, and conduct."[4] This transformation is brought about by the indwelling of the Spirit of God, which means that only those who have been regenerated by the Spirit of God can be renewed in their thinking, for the unregenerate has

---

3. J.A. Fitzmyer, S.J. ed., *Romans: A New Translation with Introduction and Commentary* (London, UK.: Yale University Press, 2008), 641.

4. Ibid.

no indwelling of the Spirit of God and is therefore ruled by the passions of the body (his sinful nature), while those who have been regenerated by the Spirit of God have "the mind of Christ".[5]

What does this mean more practically? That the regenerate does not think like the unregenerate, or that he ought not to. We do not, after all, think in such a way that is completely free from the fallen influence of this world, but we should be ever striving towards attaining that fully renewed mind in Christ, for that is what is taking place in us, we are being renewed until the day Christ returns. Now, I should clarify, the term "mind" used here by Paul is not solely confined to intellectual pursuits, it also includes "an important moral element".[6] Remember what I had written previously as to the different components that comprise a philosophical system, these are epistemology, metaphysics/ontology, and ethics/morality. These three components are presupposed by Paul's writing here, for to have a renewed mind means to have *knowledge* (or wisdom) that was not previously accessible when in an unregenerate state, and this knowledge concerns our *being* and that of *everything* else in creational (cosmic) reality, and this knowledge is religiously vertically oriented in worship of our Creator God, which thus determines the *ethical/moral* direction of our living, which is in stark contrast to the unregenerate's horizontally oriented worship of creation.

What is the purpose of this *renewed* mind? The term

---

5. Ibid., 642.

6. Leon Morris, *The Pillar New Testament Commentary: The Epistle to the Romans* (Grand Rapids, MI.: Wm. B. Eerdmans, 1988), 435.

"test" does not adequately communicate what is meant here by Paul. He does not mean to be able to test, as in prove true or false, whether the will of God is "good, pleasing, and perfect." Instead, what is meant here is *spiritually discerning* that the will of God is in fact "good, pleasing, and perfect", and having discovered this by the illumination of the Spirit, the will of God should then be "put into practice."[7] To put it another way, commentator Leon Morris writes:

> The renewal of the mind enables the believer to discern what is good, what is pleasing to God, and what is perfect. And having discerned it, that same renewal sets him to the task of performing what is seen as the will of God.

How now does this relate to Christian philosophy? Recall what I had written in the first chapter, we *all* have a worldview, a system of beliefs, a network of presuppositions, concerning knowledge, metaphysics, and ethics, or to put it more simply, concerning creational (cosmic) reality. That worldview is undergirded by one's *supra*-rational faith, which is religious by nature because man is an inescapably religious being (we all have faith in an *ultimate*; Christians have faith in the Triune God of Christian theism, while unbelievers have faith in some aspect or absolutization of creation, again this meant in an *ultimate* sense). Philosophy, as a science (or discipline), as a *theoretical enterprise*, is not independent to worldview, just as theology or any another science is not independent. Philosophy is *subject* to a person's worldview.

If we, therefore, who are in Christ, have *renewed minds* as a result of the work of the Spirit of God, this renewal will be reflected in our respective worldview. And while

---

7. Ibid.

our worldview will not be entirely faithful to the parameters provided by the Word of God, due to the noetic effects of sin which we have not been entirely freed from yet, it will nonetheless demonstrate a certain degree of faithfulness that we could without a doubt ascertain as being a *Christian* worldview. Let me explain it this way, when the Spirit of God performs the work of regeneration in a person's heart, and as a result that person repents of their sin and surrenders their life to the Lordship of Christ in response to the irresistible grace of God, what happens in that moment is a renewal of the person's mind. I would go as far as to say that the renewal took place at the same time as the regeneration of the heart, for the Old Testament Judaic understanding of the heart is not in reference to the organ or the emotions, but to the central root-unity of man, the "I". And while the state of the renewed heart when compared to the previous unregenerate state is like comparing day and night, the renewal of the heart, and therefore of the mind, is a continual process until we "become mature, attaining to the *whole* measure of the *fullness* of Christ" (Eph. 4:13). Thus a newly regenerated person will have a worldview that has begun to be shaped by the person's limited understanding of the gospel and the Word of God, and as that person grows in his knowledge of God and His Word, his worldview will continue to undergo *reformation* as a result of his continual *renewal* by the Spirit of God.

I would love to be able to say that I myself have a *perfectly* biblical worldview, and not just in the sense of understanding Scripture, but how it relates to every aspect of life, but the truth is that I will never have a *perfectly* biblical worldview. I am a fallible and errant being who continues to be, though to a lesser extent, impeded by the noetic effects of sin, and that will remain the case until the day Christ returns and I am fully renewed along with the rest of creation. Should I, therefore, give up pursuing a *perfectly* biblical worldview? I think such an objective is unattainable and unrealistic as long as we live in this fallen world, and as long as we remain subject to the fallenness, though we are destined in Christ for complete redemption. However, the same could be said for becoming mature in the sense of attaining "the whole measure of the fullness of Christ" (Eph. 4:13). Should I, therefore, give that up as well? Absolutely not. I should strive, and continue to strive, for such a God-glorifying maturity, for a right understanding of creational (cosmic) reality, until the day Christ returns, for we are all in Christ called to persevere in our walk of faith as we await that great climax of creational (cosmic) history when all things are renewed in the One who holds all things together (Col. 1:17). Is it unattainable and unrealistic as long as we live in this fallen world? Within that limited context, yes. But, it is not unattainable and unrealistic when we take eternity into consideration, because when we factor in Christ's second advent, that which is unattainable and unrealistic becomes attainable and realistic, and I am referring here to both a right understanding of creational (cosmic) reality and the Christ-like maturity that Paul mentions in Ephesians 4:13.

Why is it important that we reform our worldview according to the teachings of the Bible? Recall, again, that I mentioned that the Bible was not a textbook for the natural sciences, or any other science (or discipline) for that matter, but rather that it provides the building blocks for a *Christian* worldview, which makes it less specialized (limited) than it if were to be a textbook, and more foundational (expansive) in that it informs all of the sciences and everything else that man does under the sun. The Bible is God's special revelation unto man, the only authoritative interpretation of creational (cosmic) reality, God's general revelation. In truth, it speaks towards man's relationship with God, man's relationship with fellow man, and man's relationship to the rest of creation. To understand why we must continually *reform* our worldview as our minds are continually *renewed*, and to be more specific, why we must have a *Christian* philosophy that stems from this worldview – for how can we logically have a Christian worldview and not a Christian understanding of the sciences (or disciplines)? – we must understand the calling of man in the light of creation, fall, and redemption.

5.2 The Calling of Man

What was the calling of man when he was created? When man was created in the Garden of Eden, he was called to be God's prophet, priest, and king. The historical Adam, therefore, who was created by God out of the dust, and the historical Eve, who was created by God out of Adam's rib, were God's prophets, priests, and kings (in Eve's case, it would be more appropriate to say "queen", not only in regard to her biological identity, but also in regard to her place under Adam as his wife). What did it mean for man to be God's prophet? The Christian thinker, and student of Dooyeweerd, R.J. Rushdoony (1916-2001), wrote:

> A prophet is one who speaks God's word and interprets the world and its events in terms of God's law. The prophet role

of man, therefore, as given to Adam, was to develop the world and to interpret it, to analyze it, to study it in terms of God's word.[8]

To put it more simply, man was to interpret and articulate creational (cosmic) reality according to the revelation of God in every respect. As a creature of God, uniquely created in the image of God, man was to presuppose in all his living and thinking that he lived in God's world, that all came from the hand of the Creator, and that all of creational (cosmic) reality was subject to God's law-word, and thus, subject to God's sovereign reign. We might put it another way: God's *propositional* revelation was to serve as the lens by which man might view and interpret the world so that God's truths may be known and embraced. In this respect, we are referring to the construction of a worldview (the lens) using the building blocks provided by God's revelation.

But the calling of man to be God's prophet is not independent from the other two offices of priest and king. What did it mean for man to be God's priest? To be God's priest meant to dedicate, to *consecrate*, the whole of creational (cosmic) reality, along with himself, in service to the living God through his cultural work.[9] Prior to addressing the matter of "culture" and "cultural work", however, let me first briefly comment on the relationship between the offices of prophet and priest. It follows logically that if man lives out what he interprets of creational (cosmic) reality as God's

---

8. R.J. Rushdoony, "Salvation and Godly Rule: Prophet, Priest & King", *Pocket College*. Accessed November 5, 2021, http://www.pocketcollege.com/transcripts/091%20-%20Salvation%20and%20Godly%20Rule/RR136AG62.html/.

9. Ibid.

prophet, then he can do nothing less but dedicate creational (cosmic) reality unto God through this living out of his interpretation as God's priest. Remember, *nothing* that man does under the sun can be considered *irreligious*, everything that he thinks and acts always has a religious *direction*, and thus for Adam and Eve, all that they did was in worship to the Creator God as His priests.

Was man to simply interpret and articulate (as prophets), and dedicate and consecrate (as priests) creational (cosmic) reality? No, he was also to govern and rule as God's vice-regent, as God's king, over all creational (cosmic) reality, bringing all things within his dominion under the sway of God's law-word (Gen. 1:28). The creation of the world was not some blank slate for man to make whatever he willed without any guiding principle, creation was instead purposed since time immemorial by the Creator God to be *His* kingdom, and the glory of that kingdom was to be developed by man subject to God in terms of God's divine purpose.

5.3 The Cultural Mandate

This brings us to the purpose, to the objective, of man's threefold calling, which we find in Genesis 1:26-28.

> Then God said, "Let us make man in our image, after our likeness. And let them have dominion over the fish of the sea and over the birds of the heavens and over the livestock and over all the earth and over every creeping thing that creeps on the earth."
>
> So God created man in his own image,
>   in the image of God he created him;
>   male and female he created them.

And God blessed them. And God said to them, "Be fruitful and multiply and fill the earth and subdue it, and have dominion over the fish of the sea and over the birds of the heavens and over every living thing that moves on the earth."

Theologians have called this passage the "cultural mandate", in that man was not called merely to multiply and fill the earth, but to also exercise *dominion* over the creational domain that was placed under him, cultivating creation into a God-glorifying civilization. This is how we can understand culture and man's relation to it: *Culture is man's cultivation of creation, which has a religious nature to it given man's religiousity.* As Christian thinker and cultural analyst P. Andrew Sandlin writes: "Creation is what God makes; culture is what we make. Culture is quite different from creation; its distinctive trait is the human use of that creation for man's benefit."[10] And we are further enlightened by the writings of Boot:

> The English words *culture* and *agriculture* are derived from a Latin root (*colere*) and are related to *cultus* (worship). The direct association of culture with worship is most noticeable in our ongoing use of the word cult for various religions. Culture is perhaps best understood as the *public manifestation of the religious ground-motive (i.e. worship) of a people.* Culture is therefore a state of being cultivated by intellectual and moral tilling in terms of a prevailing *cultus* and, by natural extension, forms a particular type of civilization.[11]

---

10. P. Andrew Sandlin, *Christian Culture: An Introduction* (Mount Hermon, CA.: Center for Cultural Leadership, 2013), 21.

11. Joseph Boot, *Gospel Culture: Living in God's Kingdom* (Toronto, ON.: Ezra Press, 2016), 3.

Man, therefore, was called since the beginning to *cultivate creation into a godly civilization (culture)*. How was man to fulfill this divine cultural mandate? As God's prophet, priest, and king.

5.4 Vice-Regent or Vice-Gerent?

Prior to proceeding any further, a clarification must be made in regard to the reference of man as God's *vice-regent*. A student of H. Evan Runner, John Hultink, once explained that under Runner there was an issue with the term "vice-regent", writing:

> A vice-regent... is someone who acts in the place of a ruler, like the vice-president of the United States who acts in the place of the president when he is unconscious or dead. We do not act in God's place. God is sovereign; always present, always sovereign. Christians are always and everywhere God's vice-gerents. All our authority, all our power, is delegated to us by God, who is the ruler and supreme head. So we do not act in God's place, for God has not relinquished His sovereignty, nor, contrary to public academic opinion, is God dead; our human acts are always and everywhere acts in response to the mandate God has delegated us to perform. CORAM DEO! So you see... we are God's vice-gerents; not His vice-regents.[12]

The distinction that Runner makes is valid in terms of man's relationship to God and how it manifests in his functioning, but, it should be noted, those who use the term "vice-regent" within reformational circles are not presupposing that man rules in God's place, but rather, presup-

---

12. Cited in John Hultink, "H. Evan Runner: Man of God", *Christian Renewal* (2003), 3.

posing the meaning of vice-gerent. Why do I not use the term vice-gerent? Because while vice-gerent means "a person appointed to exercise all or some of the authority of another," and to be "delegated authority",[13] the term vice-regent can *also* mean to act as a "representative" or as an "assistant" to a higher authority.[14] So while Runner believes that the distinction of terms should be made, since vice-regent can be interpreted as man ruling as God's substitute, as if God were somehow absent or dead, that is not how I am referring to the term. I am not the only one to use this term in this way in fact. Consider, for example, Rushdoony, who says that given that the term "vice-regent" is being meant in the *biblical* sense, "A vice-gerent and a vice-regent, they are both essentially the same thing... different terms, but the same thing."[15] Joe Boot, a rising contemporary Christian thinker, well versed in Dooyeweerdian philosophy in addition to his reformed theology, likewise uses the term "vice-regent."[16] So there is nothing wrong with the use of the term in reference to man as God's king, so long as we understand it in light of God's special written revelation.

13. "Vice Gerent", *Collins*. Accessed November 2, 2021, https://www.collinsdictionary.com/dictionary/english/vicegerent/.

14. "Vice Regent", *Collins*. Accessed November 2, 2021, https://www.collinsdictionary.com/dictionary/english/viceregent/.

15. R.J. Rushdoony, "Systematic Theology – Sin", *Pocket College*. Accessed November 4, 2021, https://pocketcollege.com/transcripts/111%20-%20Systematic%20Theology%20-%20Sin/RR4092b.html/.

16. Cf. Joe Boot, "Ministry, Service, and Power", *Ezra Institute*. Accessed November 1, 2021, https://www.ezrainstitute.ca/resource-library/sermons/ministry-service-and-power/.

5.5 Prophet, Priest, and King

Returning to the purpose, the objective, of man's threefold office as prophet, priest, and king, which was for the fulfillment of the cultural mandate, the reformed theologian Herman Bavinck (1854-1921) had this to say:

> Gen. 1:26 teaches us that God had a purpose in creating man in His image: namely, that man should *have dominion*… If now we comprehend the force of this subduing (dominion) under the term of *culture*… we can say that *culture in its broadest sense is the purpose for which God created man after his image*.[17]

Of course, the fall of man presented a real problem, for while it was expected for man to fulfill the cultural mandate without the corrupting influence of sin, when man did sin, when Eve, and then Adam, ate the fruit from the forbidden tree of knowledge, all went awry under the sun. To clarify, there was nothing special about this tree, in the sense that it did not possess any supernatural qualities that would have differentiated it from all other trees. It was an ordinary tree, and needed to be so, in order that by honouring and obeying God in respect to this tree man might learn how to honour and obey God in respect to the rest of creation. If this tree was special, it was only special in the sense that it was the only tree that bore fruit that was forbidden for man to consume. However, what can be said is that this fall did have a *radical* impact on man, creation, and his functioning under the fixed law-order. What was man's original sin? To

---

17   Herman Bavinck, "The Origin, Essence and Purpose of Man," in *Selected Shorter Works of Herman Bavinck*, John Hendryx, ed. (West Linn, OR.: Monergism Books, 2015), loc. 469.

have eaten the forbidden fruit of the tree of knowledge? It is much more profound, and far more sinister than that. It was man's desire, prompted by the crafty serpent, the deceiver, to be like God in a way that was inappropriate for a creature, to be radically autonomous, totally independent from God epistemically, metaphysically/ontologically, and ethically/ morally. It was not the tree of knowledge that bequeathed man with the knowledge of good and evil, man came to learn evil by committing evil, and thus learning the stark contrast between good and evil.

As a result of man's sin, all of creation was placed under the curse of sin, and thus the world has, ever since, appeared as in need of redemption, it appears *fallen*. How could man, thus, cultivate creation into a godly civilization? How could he fulfill the cultural mandate? With sin having entered the picture, the glorious realization of this mandate became an impossibility for man alone. But this did not mean that his calling as prophet, priest, and king were negated. The calling is itself evident in man's created nature, it was what he was created to do, and thus, in his sin and since the fall, the natural (unregenerate) man, in his apostate state, has served as his own prophet, priest, and king. As his own prophet, he has rejected the true knowledge of God in favour of an illusion, the exchange of God as the ultimate starting point for all thought for some aspect of creation, an exchange which man has been falsely led to believe would result in his desired deification. As the theologian Geerhardus Vos (1862-1949) rightly noted, the effect of sin on the totality of man resulted in his "radical reversal," whereas before man was created originally upright and in close communion with the living God, sin has ravaged his being and has disrupted his communion with God by reorienting the direction of his worship towards that of creation, resulting in his spiritual depravation, disorganization, and decomposition.[18] The natural man thus interprets creational (cosmic) reality, not according to God's law-word, but according to his own vain, finite, baseless and fallen thought. As his own priest, man dedicates everything unto himself, putting the whole world, that is, every person and thing in creational (cosmic) reality, to his own service. And having done so, even to this day, has made all things *profanos*, Greek for "living, speaking, thinking… outside of God," as Rushdoony writes, "any kind of speaking, living or acting outside of God is profane."[19] As his own king, man props up through his cultural work his own kingdom, marked by sin and apostasy, and in direct opposition to the sovereign rule of God. Epistemology, metaphysics/ontology, ethics/morality, become subject to man's redefinition in this godless, humanistic kingdom. The natural man, under the sway of his sinful disposition, is led to believe that *he* can be the measure of all things, but what this pursuit accomplishes is nothing more than the casting of man into his lightless abyss of purposelessness and meaninglessness.

Has man, thus, been rendered incapable of fulfilling the cultural mandate since the fall? Not at all, for neither the adversary that spoke through the serpent, nor the natural man, has the last say in the history of creational (cosmic) reality. When God sent us His Son, Jesus the Christ, the earth

18. Geerhardus Vos, *Reformed Dogmatics, Vol. Two: Anthropology*, ed., trans., Richard B. Gaffin, Jr., et al. (Grand Rapids, MI.: Lexham Press, 2012), 14.

19. Rushdoony, "Salvation and Godly Rule: Prophet, Priest & King".

received the "last Adam" (1 Cor. 15:22), through whom all those who were dead in their sin and awaiting judgement would be brought to life and redeemed by His saving grace and will. This last Adam, the Christ, graced this earth in bodily form as both fully God and fully man, and being both divine and human in nature, free from the sin that has ransacked humanity, He came as God's Prophet, Priest, and King. Alluding to His prophetic office, He proclaimed the law and the gospel as absolute and exclusive truth (Matt. 5), speaking as one having authority, for all things within creation obeyed His command (Mark 1:22; 4:41; Luke 4:32). Having come into the world to testify of the truth (John 18:37), He called himself a King, and with miraculous signs and wonders He confirms, even to this day, the veracity and authority of His teaching (John 2:11; 10:37), communicating not only the legitimacy of His royal power (Matt. 9:6, 8; 21:23) but also His priestly compassion (Matt. 8:17). The gospel records of the New Testament do not merely record Christ as having performed the functions of a prophet, priest and king, but as also being in His entirety *the* Prophet, Priest and King, operating even today. As Boot writes:

> In the midst of man's futile efforts to remake himself as divine (as his own god), in the purposes of God, at the right moment, God sent forth the seed of the woman, his own Son the Messiah as the *second Adam* (1 Cor. 15:45-48), to be the true *office-bearer* and so embody the office that man had been called to fulfill in the beginning. Jesus does this by perfect obedience. Christ therefore is situated in the gospel story as the one who *restores God's order*, bringing all things back to God by redeeming his new people, or new humanity... In life, the Messiah not only fulfills the *cultural role* of prophet,

priest, and king, just as Adam was called to do in the garden, but by his atoning death, he purchased *the right of renewal* of a new people, re-commissioned to be prophets, priests and kings in the service of God and to be his co-workers in the power of the Spirit, in the reconciling of all things in heaven and earth to God.[20]

Yes, you read that correctly, in *the* Prophet, Priest, and King, in Jesus Christ, the cultural mandate is renewed within the context of the Great Commission:

> …All authority in heaven and on earth has been given to me. Go therefore and make disciples of all nations, baptizing them in the name of the Father and of the Son and of the Holy Spirit, teaching them to observe all that I have commanded you. And behold, I am with you always, to the end of the age (Matt. 28:18-20).

Man has thus *not* been rendered incapable of fulfilling the cultural mandate, because it is God who has the final say in the history of creational (cosmic) reality, and He has determined since eternity past for man to fulfill this cultural mandate under and in the Son and through His gospel renewing work. For the gospel is not merely the *salvation* from sin, though that is the core, the kernel of the gospel, but also the being *brought into* the kingdom of God to serve His divine purpose as His image-bearers and office-bearers.[21]

5.6 The Vitality of a Christian Philosophy for the Cultural Mandate

In light of all this, we must now ask, How does a distinctly

---

20. Boot, *Gospel Culture*, 96.
21. Ibid., 97.

Christian philosophy help us in fulfilling the cultural mandate? Well, for starters, Christian philosophy provides with a right and true understanding of creational (cosmic) reality. For example, it helps us to distinguish between *structure* and *direction* in creational (cosmic) reality, a necessary distinction as we will see, and for this concept we can thank Dooyeweerd's brother-in-law, D.H. Th. Vollenhoven.[22] The term "structure" is in reference to creational structures, or the "structural laws that God has instituted for the various creatures and cosmic modalities", as per Willem J. Ouweneel, and "direction" is in reference to the "directedness of any entity, event, or state of affairs."[23] As you can already surmise, there are only two directions – I have already employed this term of "direction" in this manner –, either it is in the vertical orientation (or positive direction) toward the Creator God and His honour, or in the horizontal orientation (apostate direction) toward creation, which is thus away from the Creator and toward His dishonour. I sometimes refer to a person's *worldview* as structural, given that it is in and of itself a structure, otherwise it could not be a systematic worldview, and it would not be wrong to employ this term in this way, and in terms of a person's *religion*, I refer to that as directional. Thus, when I use the term "religious worldview" in several of my writings and lectures, I mean the *direction* (religion) of that *structure* (worldview).

If we hope to meaningfully participate in the redemp-

22. Cf. J. Glenn Friesen, "D.H. Th. Vollenhoven", *Christian Nondualism*. Accessed November 2, 2021, https://jgfriesen.wordpress.com/d-h-th-vollenhoven/.

23. Willem J. Ouweneel, *Wisdom for Thinkers: Introduction to Christian Philosophy* (Jordan Station, ON.: Paideia Press, 2014), 76-77.

tion of all things, not as the one who redeems – for that is alone the work of God –, but as those who have been invited by God's grace to participate in this redemption work by means of gospel proclamation and application, the latter of which includes the fulfillment of the cultural mandate, then we need a right understanding of creational (cosmic) reality, and the more we learn and know, the better. For how else can we work towards cultural renewal if we have no understanding, that is, no *right* understanding, of what creational (cosmic) reality is and what it should be, either as a whole or in its varied aspects? When I say "should be", I am not referring to the structural dimension of creation, in terms of the fixed law-order. While all of creation has been made subject to the curse of sin (Gen. 3:17-19; Rom. 8:20), the creational law-order was never affected, for otherwise sin would have destroyed the creational order and this would have affected God's sovereignty by, believe it or not, asserting the autonomous role of Satan over against God.[24] Thus, to assert that sin changed the fixed law-order would be tantamount to heresy. What the Word of God reveals to us is that this is not at all the case, what sin affected was *not* the structural dimension of creational (cosmic) reality, but "the functioning of creatures under these ordinances."[25] So when I say: "what creational (cosmic) reality *should be*", I mean what it should be in regard to man's *functioning* under the fixed law-order. You can begin to grasp how vitally important it is then that we have a *Christian* philosophy, a *Christian* understanding of epistemology, metaphysics/ontology, and ethics/morality, of creational (cosmic) reality. And in truth, what

---

24. Ouweneel, *Wisdom for Thinkers*, 77.
25. Ibid.

could possibly take its place when we live and breathe in God's world? Therefore, only a philosophy that is *informed* by the unified revelation (special + general) of God, that stems from a *Christian*, biblical worldview, can supply us with a roadmap in advancing in our efforts towards arriving at cultural renewal and reformation, in fulfillment of our threefold calling as God's prophets, priests, and kings. As Christian thinker Josué Reichow explains, the Dooyeweerdian Christian philosophical system

> assumes that reality is *meaning*, given as a gift from the Creator. This meaning is like the sunlight refracted through a prism, scattering into different colours and nuances, but coming from the same source... Humans experience this meaning in *different modes*, without qualitatively differentiating them before theoretical abstraction. "For each aspect, particular *laws* or *norms* are found" (Kalsbeek, *Contornos da filosofia crista*, p. 38). This analogy explains how Christ's sovereignty is expressed in the world. God has a single will, perfect and consistent. However, when his will "crosses" the prism of time, it is expressed in different laws. Each law, in the creation of God, can be compared to one of the colours of the spectrum of light.[26]

As God's prophets, we are to interpret reality according to God's law-word. As God's priests, we are to dedicate and consecrate creation and all our interaction with it as a form of worship unto God and to His service. And as God's kings, we are to govern this world subject to the righteous and sovereign rule of God. All this is made possible by Christ,

---

26. Josué Reichow, *Reformai a vossa mente: A filosofia cristã de Herman Dooyeweerd*, Kindle Edition (Brazil: Editora Monergismo, 2019) Loc. 1895.

and what a distinctly *Christian* philosophy manages to accomplish is to make this fulfillment all the easier. To clarify, I do not mean that this work is in any way *easy*, history testifies to the contrary since the conception of the church, but rather that this work is more easily accomplished *with* a Christian philosophy than without one, for without one we will only be walking in circles, never making any true progress due to the various parasitic pagan syntheses that pollutes our minds and therefore our missional efforts.

5.7 The Vitality of a Christian Philosophy for Christian Living

We return again to the thought of the international missionaries working in red zone areas, in impoverished and illiterate communities, and of the humble believers in third-world countries. We could even extend our thought to the average-Joe, everyday Christian that we find all across the globe. Of what benefit would a Christian philosophy serve them? How might we understand the vitality of Christian philosophy for Christian living? That is to say, for our living *Coram Deo*, Latin for "in the presence of God".

First, consider what the apostle Paul wrote to the Roman church:

> Do not be conformed to this world, but be transformed by the renewal of your mind, that by testing you may discern what is the will of God, what is good and acceptable and perfect (Rom. 12:2).

Paul is saying that we as Christians are not to be conformed to this world in terms of how we *live*, we are to live *Christianly*, that is to say, in accordance with the teach-

95

ings of Jesus and the rest of written revelation (the Bible). And how we live is for the most part determined by how we *think*. And what does Paul say? That we must be "transformed by the renewal of your mind." When we talk about the renewal of the human person in Christ, we are referring to the purging of all that is antithetical to the perfection of Christ, namely, sin and its corruptive influence, and the restoration of the *imago Dei* which had been marred by sin. That is what we call "regeneration", which is the work of the Spirit of God. This includes our minds, our intellect, our thinking. Thus, to renew our minds involves then the purging of all that is antithetical to the knowledge (wisdom) of Christ, and the restoration of our right understanding of creational (cosmic) reality. Though the following analogy is limited, it nonetheless helps to illustrate what this renewing of our minds implies. Think of a computer system, what happens when it becomes infected by a virus? The damage can be catastrophic. Sin is much like a virus. And regeneration is much like a virus being purged from the computer system while it is being restored. Our minds still have remnants of fallen thought that need to be altogether cleaned out, but in order to purge them from our thinking, we need to substitute it with renewed thinking (i.e., kicking Darwinian evolution to the curb and replacing it with a biblical understanding of origins as it relates to life).

Second, without a Christian philosophy, missionaries – and that includes *all* Christians who are called to serve missionally in every aspect of their lives – can only have a general understanding of what they are working toward, and many times this general understanding is severely lacking. Think, for example, of the common Christian misconception that the missional role of the Christian is simply that of seeking after the spiritual salvation of people's souls for entry into heaven. This is what we might refer to as a truncation of the gospel, because it fails to understand the full scope and extent of the gospel (and the Lordship of Christ) by reducing it to soteriology (salvation) alone. What about the restoration of creation? And by that, I do not just mean the restoration of creation from its state of fallenness, I mean the restoration of man's functioning. Many Christians shunt that off to the future and resign themselves from working towards restoration in this sense because their minds have been polluted by pagan syntheses, whether this be dualistic Gnosticism, the retreatist Dispensationalism of the Plymouth Brethren, unbiblical Fatalism, the artificial sacred-secular divide, etc. A Christian philosophy provides missional believers with a more comprehensive understanding of what they are working towards, a map of sorts towards wholistic gospel restoration. For example, in reference to norms (distinct from the laws of nature), it provides the believer with an understanding of God's original design for human functioning from the sixth to the fifteenth modal lawsphere. What was God's design for human functioning in the psychical (sense, feeling, emotion, perception), analytical (logic, distinction, conceptualization), historical (formative, deliberate shaping, history, culture, technology, objectives, achievement), lingual (meaning carried by symbols), social (community, sociality, relationships, roles, respect), economic (frugal management of resources, stewardship), aesthetic (harmony, recreational play, enjoyment), juridical (responsibilities and rights), ethical (self-giving love, generousity), and pistical (vision, aspiration, commitment, belief) aspects? How has *sin* affected man's functioning in these aspects? And what would restoration look like through gospel renewal?[27]

You might quip back, "But God has never been hampered from accomplishing His redemptive purposes through His people in the Old and New Testaments and throughout the history of the Church because of a lack of a Christian philosophy amongst His people." You are right, praise God for that, but let me say two things: (1) God accomplishes His redemptive purposes through His people *in spite* of us, *not* because of us; and (2) It is an *expectation* that the people of God grow in maturity and wisdom through the ages, instructed by the Word of God, illuminated by the Spirit of God, and guided by the maturity and wisdom of the saints that came before us. If we were to dismiss Christian philosophy for that reason, we may as well abandon every advancement in the natural sciences and limit ourselves to the most basic understanding of the Israelites of the Old Testament. Why stop there? What is the most basic form of intelligence in human history that we could reduce our thinking and living to? You get the point. As God accomplishes His redemptive purposes, as He works towards restoring creation through gospel renewal, God's people are to be continually progressing, not regressing, in their wholistic development as their minds are continually renewed. Christian philosophy is not optional for the Christian believer – that is certainly how some have treated it, while others have dismissed it as not even being an option at all (mainly, irrationalists, anti-intellectualists, and those who have bought into the artificial sacred-secular divide). On the contrary, Christian

---

27. Ouweneel, *Wisdom for Thinkers*, 78.

philosophy is *vital* for our Christian living, for our living *Coram Deo.*

ABOUT THE AUTHOR

STEVEN R. MARTINS is a Christian thinker and writer, founding director of the Cántaro Institute and founding pastor of Sevilla Chapel in St. Catharines, ON. He has worked in the fields of missional apologetics and church leadership for ten years and has spoken at numerous conferences, churches, and University student events. He has also served as the Project Manager of Paideia Press and contributed articles to *Coalición por el Evangelio* (TGC in Spanish) and the *Siglo XXI* journal of Editorial CLIR. Steven holds a Master's degree *summa cum laude* in Theological Studies with a focus on Christian apologetics from Veritas International University (Santa Ana, CA., USA) and a Bachelor of Human Resource Management from York University (Toronto, ON., Canada). Steven is married to Cindy and they live in Lincoln, Ontario, with their sons Matthias, Timothy, and Nehemías.

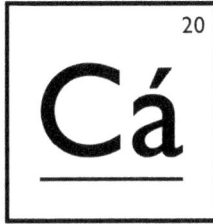

About the Cántaro Institute
Inheriting, Informing, Inspiring

The Cántaro Institute is a confessional evangelical Christian organization established in 2020 that seeks to recover the riches of Spanish Protestantism for the renewal and edification of the contemporary church and to advance the comprehensive Christian philosophy of life for the religious reformation of the Western and Ibero-American world.

We believe that as the Christian church returns to the fount of Scripture as her ultimate authority for all knowing and living, and wisely applies God's truth to every aspect of life, faithful in spirit to the reformers, her missiological activity will result in not only the renewal of the human person but also the reformation of culture, an inevitable result when the true scope and nature of the gospel is made known and applied.

CPSIA information can be obtained
at www.ICGtesting.com
Printed in the USA
BVHW031006060922
646251BV00019B/810

9 781990 771033